A STRAIGHTFORWARD GUIDE
TO
BUYING, SELLING AND
RENTING OUT YOUR PROPERTY

Frank Worth

Editor: Roger Sproston

Straightforward Publishing

D1392266

British cataloguing in Publication Data. A Catalogue record of this publication is available in the British Library.

ISBN:
978-1-84716-935-8

4edge www.4edge.co.uk

Cover design by Bookworks Islington

Whilst every effort has been taken to ensure that the information contained within this book is correct at the time of going to press, the publisher and author cannot be held responsible for any errors or omissions contained within or for any subsequent changes in the law.

CONTENTS

Introduction

Chapter 1 –Buying a Home-Looking for a Home   16

Chapter 2-The Role of Estate Agents in Buying and Selling Property

Chapter 5-Selling Your Home   73

Chapter 6-Conveyancing a Property   81

****

INTRODUCTION

As time goes by, we either find ourselves in the middle of a housing market 'boom' or a 'bust'. Currently, at the time of writing, **2019,** we are experiencing an erratic cycle in house prices, the London market is growing in certain areas and contracting in others due, it is said, to a lack of new housing. Whatever the cause, home ownership is beyond the reach of many in the South East generally. Other areas outside of London and the South East are showing signs of growth..

However, notwithstanding market conditions, the process of buying and selling a home remains probably the single most important activity undertaken by individuals in their lifetime. The money and effort involved means that it is a process that must be carried out effectively and with a clear knowledge of the elements involved.

There are different people out there buying property, some private individuals and other buy-to-let investors. This book is aimed generally at those who are trying to buy and sell a property, and is also aimed at those who wish to rent out properties, usually as 'casual landlords' as the title suggests, but also professional buy--to-let investors and indeed those who wish to be tenants..

When buying or selling a home, particularly buying, you will liase with a whole number of people, professional or otherwise: solicitors, estate agents, finance brokers, surveyors, banks and building societies and so on. All of these people play a vital role in the house purchase/sale transaction. All of these parties involved will have many years experience of property and not all of them will be acting in your own best interests.

Very often, the person who owns the property or who wishes to purchase a property is the one with the least knowledge of the process and is the one who stands to lose the most. When initially looking for a property, wrong decisions are made. The price paid for a property is quite often too high, with disastrous consequences later on. The condition of the property may leave a lot to be desired. There are many stories of people losing out on this single most important transaction. Unfortunately, it is a fact that if mistakes are made at the outset then you might spend the rest of your life recovering from the consequences.

As mentioned, this book also covers renting out a property and all that entails. The responsibilities of landlords, both the 'casual' landlord and the professional investor are considerable and it is also important to be aware of the tax and accounting implications of being a landlord, whether you are an individual with one property or are a landlord with a larger portfolio. Currently, in 2019 tax rules for landlords are changing and not favourably, which are outlined in chapter 17.

****

Chapter 1

Buying a Home-Looking for a Home

Obviously, where you choose to buy your house will be your own decision. However, it may be your first time and you may be at a loss as to where to buy, i.e. rural areas or urban areas, the type and cost of property or whether a house or flat. There are several considerations here:

Area

Buying in a built up area has its advantages and disadvantages. There are normally more close communities, because of the sheer density. However, it is true to say that some built up areas have become fragmented by population movement, "Gentrification" etc. Local services are closer to hand and there is a greater variety of housing for sale. Transport links are also usually quite good and there are normally plenty of shops.

Disadvantages are less space, less privacy, more local activity, noise and pollution, less street parking, more expensive insurance and different schooling to rural environments. The incidence of crime and vandalism and levels of overall stress are higher in built up urban areas. This is not the case with all built up areas. It is up to the buyer to carry out research before making a commitment. If you are considering buying in a rural area, you might want to consider the following: there is more detached housing with land, more space and privacy. However, this can be undermined by the "village" syndrome where everyone knows your business, or wants to know your business. There is also cleaner air and insurance premiums can be lower. Disadvantages can be isolation, loneliness, lower level of services generally, and a limited choice of local education. One really good website which helps you compare all aspects of different areas is www.onefamily.com/best-places-live-work-uk.

Choosing your property

You should think carefully when considering purchasing a larger property. You may encounter higher costs, which may include:

- Larger, more expensive, carpeting
- More furniture. It is highly unlikely that your existing furniture will suit a new larger home.
- Larger gardens to tend. Although this may have been one of the attractions, large gardens are time consuming, expensive and hard work.
- Bigger bills
- More decorating
- Higher overall maintenance costs

Valuing a property

In the main, buyers will leave it to estate agents to offer a fair price, or market price for the house. In a period of spiralling house price inflation which is now thankfully over, although there was a re-occurrence of this in London, values were seemingly plucked out of the air. If you want to compare estate agents valuations with others then you can access one of the websites, such as www.hometrack.com/uk or rightmove in order to gain a comparative value. Other sites are the Halifax, Nationwide, the Royal Institute of Chartered Surveyors, the National Association of Estate Agents and the Land Registry. You can also gain an idea of the valuation by looking in estate agents windows and assessing similar properties.

Purchasing a flat

There are some important points to remember when purchasing a flat. These are common points that are overlooked. If you purchase a flat in a block, the costs of maintenance of the flat will be your own. However, the costs of maintaining the common parts will be down to the landlord (usually) paid for by you through a service charge. There has been an awful lot of trouble with service charges, trouble between landlord and leaseholder. It has to be said that many landlords see service charges as a way of making profit over and above other income, such as ground rent, which is usually negligible after sale of a lease.

Many landlords will own the companies that carry out the work and retain the profit made by these companies. They will charge leaseholders excessively for works which are often not needed. The 1996 Housing Act (as amended by the Commonhold and Leasehold Reform Act 2002) attempts to strengthen the hand of leaseholders against unscrupulous landlords by making it very difficult indeed for landlords to take legal action for forfeiture (repossession) of a lease without first giving the leaseholder a chance to challenge the service charges.

Be very careful if you are considering buying a flat in a block – you should establish levels of service charges and look at accounts. Try to elicit information from other leaseholders. It could be that there is a leaseholders organisation, formed to manage their own service charges. This will give you direct control over contracts such as gardening, cleaning, maintenance contacts and cyclical decoration contracts. Better value for money is obtained in this way. In this case, at least you know that the levels will be fair, as no one leaseholder stands to profit.

It is important to know that under the Leasehold Reform Act 1993 as amended by the Commonhold and Leasehold Reform Act 2002 all leaseholders have the right to extend the length of their lease by a term of 90 years. For example, if your lease has 80 years left to run you can extend it to 170 Years. There is a procedure in the above Act for valuation. Leaseholders can also collectively purchase the freehold of the block. There is a procedure for doing this in the Act although it is often time consuming and can be expensive. There are advantages however, particularly when leaseholders are not satisfied with management.

In addition to service charges and length of lease, one other very important point is that of ground rents. It has been reported widely in the press that many developers are setting ground rents (annual rents) far too high, and then selling off the freehold, which jeopardises the future saleability of the property. There have been a few court cases which have forced big developers such as Wimpy to make provision for compensation. The main tip here is make sure you look at the ground rent provisions when you buy, don't invest in something that can prove difficult to sell late ron.

Viewing properties

Before you start house hunting, draw up a list of characteristics you will need from your new home, such as the number of bedrooms,

19

size of kitchen, garage, study and garden. Take the estate agents details with you when viewing. Also, take a tape measure with you. Assess the location of the property. Look at all the aspects and the surroundings. Give some thought as to the impact this will have in your future life. Assess the building, check the facing aspect of the property, i.e., north, south etc. and check the exterior carefully. Earlier, I talked about the need to be very careful when assessing a property. When you have made your mind up, a survey is essential.

If buying a house or ground floor flat, look for a damp proof course - normally about 15cm from the ground. Look for damp inside and out. Items like leaking rainwater pipes should be noted, as they can be a cause of damp. Look carefully at the windows. Are they rotten? Do they need replacing and so on. Look for any cracks. These should most certainly be investigated. A crack can be symptomatic of something worse or it can merely be surface. If you are not in a position to make this judgement then others should make it for you.

Heating is important. If the house or flat has central heating you will need to know when it was last tested. Gas central heating should be tested at least once a year.

All in all you need to remember that you cannot see everything in a house, particularly on the first visit. A great deal may be being concealed from you. In addition, your own knowledge of property may be slim. A second opinion is a must.

Buying an old house

If you are considering purchasing an older house and making improvements then there are a number of things to think about: consider whether your proposed alterations will be in keeping with the age and style of the house, and neighbouring houses, particularly in a terrace. A classic mistake is that of replacing doors and windows with unsympathetic modern products. Again, salesmen will sell you anything and quite often won't provide the correct advice. If appropriate, you should consider contacting the Victorian Society victoriansociety.org.uk or the Georgian Group georgiangroup.org.uk for advice on preserving your home. Both offer leaflets to help you carry out appropriate restoration. It is often a good idea to employ an architect or surveyor to oversee any alterations you are considering. For local contractors contact the Royal Institute of British Architects or Royal Institute of Chartered Surveyors.

Renovation grants

These may be available from local authorities, although there are stringent requirements. They are means tested and the higher your income the more you are expected to pay. For further details you should contact your local authority direct.

Disabled facilities grant

A grant may be available to adapt a property for a disabled person, for example improving access into and around the home and adapting existing facilities within it. These grants are mandatory, but a discretionary grant is available to make a property suitable for the accommodation, welfare or employment of a disabled person. A leaflet, generally entitled Help for Disabled People with Adaptation and Other works, which can be obtained from your local authority, provides basic information.

Equalities Act 2010

The Equality Act 2010, with effect from October 2010, has introduced an obligation on all landlords to ensure that, if a disabled person requests it, suitable disabled access to common parts, and within common parts is available. Again, information is available from the local authority.

Planning permission

If you are considering alterations of a significant nature, either internal or external, you may need planning permission from your local authority. You may need planning permission if you plan to change the look or external aspect of the building or if you are intending to change the use.

You are allowed to carry out some work without planning permission, so it is worth contacting the local authority. You should also ask about building regulations. These are concerned with the materials and methods of building adopted. Regulations for work carried out in conservation areas are strict. The building control department at your local authority will be able to advise you about building regulations.

Buying a listed building

Buildings of architectural or historical interest are listed by the Secretary of State for National Heritage following consultation with English Heritage, to protect them against inappropriate alteration. In Wales, buildings are listed by the Secretary of State for Wales in consultation with CADW (Heritage Wales). In Scotland, they are listed by the Secretary of State for Scotland, in consultation with Historic Scotland. If you intend to carry out work to a listed building, you are likely to need listed building consent for any internal or external work, in addition to planning permission. The conservation officer in the local planning department can provide further information.

Buildings in conservation areas

Local authorities can designate areas of special architectural or historical significance. Conservation areas are protected to ensure that their character or interest is retained. Whole towns or villages may be conservation areas or simply one particular street. Strict regulations are laid down for conservation areas. Protection includes all buildings and all types of trees that are larger than 7cm across at 1.5m above the ground. There may be limitations for putting up signs, outbuilding or items such as satellite dishes. Any developments in the area usually have to meet strict criteria, such as the use of traditional or local materials.

This also applies to property in national parks, designated Areas of Outstanding Natural Beauty and the Norfolk or Suffolk Broads.

Whether or not a property is listed or is deemed to be in a conservation area will show up when your conveyancer carries out the local authority search.

Buying a new house

There are a number of benefits to buying a new house. You have the advantages of being the first occupants. There should not be a demand for too much maintenance or DIY jobs, as the building is new. There will, however, be a defects period which usually runs for 6 months for building and 12 months for electrical mechanical. During this period you should expect minor problems, such as cracking of walls, plumbing etc, which will be the responsibility of the builder.

Energy loss will be minimal. A new house today uses 50 per cent less energy than a house built 15 years ago; consider the savings over an older property. An energy rating indicates how energy efficient a house is. The National House Building Council uses a rating scheme based on the National Energy Services Scheme, in which houses are giving a rating between 0 and 10. A house rated 10 will be very energy efficient and have very low running costs for its size. Security and safety are built in to new houses, smoke alarms are standard and security locks on doors and windows are usually included.

When the house market is slow developers usually offer incentives to buyers, such as cashback, payment of deposit etc. Sometimes they offer a part exchange scheme. These are definitely worth looking into. However, with part exchange you may not get the price you were looking for. One more important point: always check the tenure of the house-freehold or leasehold. Do try and avoid leasehold houses. The Government from 2018 onwards has banned the sale of any new leasehold houses, although some developers are trying to ignore the ban.

Building Guarantees

All new houses should be built to certain standards and qualify for one of the building industry guarantees. These building guarantees are normally essential for you to obtain a mortgage and they also make the property attractive to purchasers when you move. A typical Guarantee is the National Housebuilding Council Guarantee (NHBC).

Websites for housebuilders

Most developers have their own websites with details and picture of their developments. These include both new properties and refurbished. In addition there are several websites that specialise in new properties only.

Buying a Rented House-Right to Buy

If you rent your house from your council, you will be able to buy it at a discount under Right to Buy legislation. the current government has increased discounts in an attempt to increase the right to buy. If you live in a new town, a housing association or housing association trust, you would need to make enquiries, as many are exempt, although the government announced that it was introducing legislation to force Housing Associations to sell properties under the right to buy. A compromise has been reached where this will be voluntary. The following rules apply to the Right to Buy:

- You get a 35% discount if you've been a public sector tenant for between 3 and 5 years.
- After 5 years, the discount goes up by 2% for every extra year you've been a public sector tenant, up to a maximum of 70% – or £82,800 across England and £110,500 in London boroughs (whichever is lower).

Flats

- You get a 50% discount if you've been a public sector tenant for between 3 and 5 years.
- After 5 years, the discount goes up by 2% for every extra year you've been a public sector tenant, up to a maximum of

70% – or £82,800 across England and £110,500 in London boroughs (whichever is lower).

If your landlord has spent money on your home

Your discount will be less if your landlord has spent money building or maintaining your home:

- in the last 10 years - if your landlord built or acquired your home before 2 April 2012
- in the last 15 years - if you're buying your home through Preserved Right to Buy, or if your landlord acquired your home after 2 April 2012

You won't get any discount if your landlord has spent more money than your home is now worth.

Social Homebuy

With Social HomeBuy, you buy a share of your council or housing association home and pay rent on the rest of it.

To apply, ask your landlord for an application form.

Discounts

You'll get a discount of between £9,000 and £16,000 on the value of your home, depending on:

- where your home is

- the size of the share you're buying

If you want to buy another share in your home later on, you'll get a discount on that too.

Buying more of your home later

You must buy at least 25% of your home. You can buy more later, until you own 100%. This is called 'staircasing'.

If you buy more of your home, your rent will go down - because it's based on how much of the property you rent. Your landlord can charge rent of up to 3% of the value of their share of your home, per year.

ExampleYour home is worth £240,000 and you buy a 50% share. Your landlord charges you 3% rent on their 50% share. 3% of £120,000 is £3,600 per year. This works out at £300 per month for you to pay in rent.

Who can't apply

You can't use Social HomeBuy if:

- you have an assured shorthold tenancy

- you're being made bankrupt

- a court has ordered you to leave your home

- your landlord is taking action against you for rent arrears, anti-social behaviour or for breaking your tenancy agreement

Not all local councils or housing associations have joined the scheme. Check with your landlord to find out if they belong to the scheme and whether your home is included

Help to Buy Schemes

See chapter 4 for more details on Help to Buy and how it might benefit you.

Shared/part ownership property

There are properties available on a shared/part ownership basis, usually from housing associations. Local Authorities also provide such schemes, although rarely. The main principle is that you buy a percentage of the property, say 50% and you rent the rest, with a service charge if a flat. As time goes by you can "staircase up" to 100% ownership. This is a scheme specially designed for those who cannot meet the full cost of outright purchase in the first instance. Usually, your total monthly outgoings are smaller than they would be if you purchased outright. Social Housing providers run a range of different schemes each year, largely depending on Government requirements. For further details you should contact a large housing association in your area who will provide you with current schemes on offer and point you in the right direction.

Self-build property

Self-build is another option for obtaining a new home. However, it is time consuming and not for the faint hearted. You need to be organised and to have organised the finances and your work programme. Usually the biggest problem is finding a suitable plot of land. There is a lot of competition. It also means that you will, unless you employ an agent, be charged with supervising a number of skilled craftsmen. Self-build usually works out cheaper than buying off a developer but it is certainly not an easy option. For more information and advice check out the following websites:

www.homebuilding.co.uk

This is run by the publishers of homebuilding and renovation magazine which is the leading magazine for homebuilders. The site is magazine style with lots of articles and also a link to www.plotfinder.net. This is a recently established database of land for sale and houses to renovate. There is an annual subscription cost, currently £42 per annum (print edition) and £60 per annum print and digital (as at 2019/2020)

www.buildstore.co.uk

This site is owned by a group of venture capitalists, individuals and companies involved in the self build market. Again, there is a mix of articles and also adverts.

www.ebuild.co.uk

This site is published by specialist publisher's webguides on line. The site includes a directory of suppliers from architectural salvage to waste disposal with links to useful sites.

www.npbs.co.uk

This is the site of Norwich and Peterborough Building Society, who offer mortgages for self build projects. The loan for self-build is released in stages linked to the building of the property. It is worth checking to see if these mortgages are on offer.

****

Chapter 2

The Role of Estate Agents in Buying and Selling Property

Estate Agents

Estate agents are the normal route to buying or selling a home, although, as we will see later, online agents are offering cheaper deals for the sale or purchase of a property, many doing it for a fixed fee. Some of these agents, such as Purple Bricks have run into trouble. Many people like the 'personal touch' and use agents. Agents generally have local knowledge and people on their books looking for specific types of property. However, there are things to watch out for, particularly in London, where there is a big demand and short supply. Estate agents will often try to charge various 'fees' for services and tie people into different charges in the contract. Always demand to know the fees and be sure where you are before you enter into a contract. A good site to get advice about estate agents fees is:

www.which.co.uk/money/mortgages-and-property/home-movers/selling-a-house/estate-agent-fees-and-contracts

What to expect from an estate agent:

- Advice on the selling or asking price of a house or flat - they know the local market

- Advice on the best way to sell (or buy) and where to advertise; they should discuss an advertising budget with you

- If selling, a meeting to visit, assess and value your home and also to take down the particulars of your home. The Property Misdescriptions Act 2010, which arose out of the bad old days of the 1980's, prevents agents from using ambiguous statements to enhance the sale of the property. You should look at the points carefully as people who are disappointed after reading such a glowing report will not purchase.

- They may ask for details of recent bills, such as council tax and electricity. They should also be willing to give advice on fixtures and fittings included in the sale.

- They should be willing to show potential buyers around your home if you are not available.

- Don't expect to have to pay for a for-sale board although some lenders will try to make a charge.

Although a seller does not have any specific duty to disclose information about a property, estate agents have specific legal obligations not to mislead members of the public.

Since 2014 agents have been covered by the general duties owed by other businesses to consumers that are set out in the Consumer Protection from Unfair Trading Regulations 2008 as amended by the Consumer Protection (Amendment) Regulations 2014 (CPRs). These regulations include a ban on misleading statements or omissions and they effectively require estate agents to reveal any material facts about a property to potential buyers.

Choosing an agent if selling

Consider the following points:

- They ought to sell your type of property or specialise in one particular area of the market
- They should be a member of one of the professional bodies such as the National Association of Estate Agents, the Royal Institution of Chartered Surveyors, The Incorporated Society of Valuers and Auctioneers, The Architects and Surveyors Institute or the Association of Building Engineers.. Obtain quotes of fees, including the basic charge and any extras you might have to pay for, such as advertising in specialist publications.

Choose at least two agents to value the house, if instructing an agent.

Sole agency selling.

Offering an agent sole agency may reduce the fee. This can be done for a limited time. After this you can instruct multiple agents. With sole agency you can sell privately, although you may still be liable for the sole agent's fee.

Joint sole agents

With this arrangement, two or more agents co-operate in the house sale and split the commission. The agents may charge a higher commission in this case.

Multiple agency

This means that you have several agents trying to sell your home, but only pay the agent who sells your property.

Buying property using the internet

There are a number of websites that also detail properties, some are independent and some are owned by the large players.

The following are a selection of the main sites:

www.rightmove.co.uk.

This is one of the largest sites, jointly owned and run by Halifax, Royal Sun Alliance, Connell and Countryside assured Group. They jointly claim to represent more than 170,000 properties covering 99% of UK postcodes. The main function of this site is as a property search site, enabling people to search for property by name of area and postcode.

Each property has a reference number and will have a photo and details. These can be obtained by clicking on the property. There is much useful information, including room sizes.

www.zoopla.co.uk

The claims of this website are that it can help the buyer to find a property, move home and settle in.

www.primelocation.co.uk

This site was launched in 2000 by a consortium of estate agents. This site deals with more expensive properties.

Selling property using the internet

Although estate agents are still the main avenues for selling property, as we have seen, the web now plays a more significant part. In addition to the websites detailed, almost all agents now have their own website. This is really an electronic shop window where your property is displayed. Buyers interested in your property should be able to e-mail the estate agent directly for a viewing.

Ten top tips when selling a property

If you are selling a property, there are a number of things that you need to get right in order to ensure the best chance on the market:

- Get the price right-this is absolutely crucial-if you try to overprice then you will harm your chances of a sale as you will lose the trust of would-be purchasers-pitch the price attractively.
- Make your property presentable-remember that you are selling your home and you should show it to its best advantage.
- get the photos right
- make sure it is described fully-do not mss anything out.
- make your agent work for you. the first 30 days on the property market are crucial. make sure you are in regular contact with
- them.
- Don't forget to include a floor plan.
- make sure you have all the relevant certificates and paperwork, such as gas and electricity certificates, and damp proofing etc.

This advice applies whether you are using a traditional high street agent or are using an online agent. make sure that what you are selling is shown in its best light.

****

Chapter 3

Buying a Property-The Practicalities

Considerations when buying a house or flat

Budgeting

Before beginning to look for a house you need to sit down and give careful thought to the costs involved in the whole process. The starting point is to identify the different elements in the overall transaction.

Deposits

Sometimes the estate agent will ask you for a small deposit when you make the offer (see Estate Agents, chapter 2). This indicates that you are serious about the offer and is a widespread and legitimate practice, as long as the deposit is not too much, £100 is usual. The main deposit for the property, i.e., the difference between the mortgage and what has been accepted for the property, isn't paid until the exchange of contracts. Once you have exchanged contracts on a property the purchase is legally binding. Until then, you are free to withdraw. The deposit cannot be reclaimed after exchange.

The main rule of thumb is that less you borrow the more favourable terms you can normally get from bank or building society. It has to be said that in the period leading up to the 'credit crunch' in 2008, we were in a situation where banks loaned money to all and sundry at up to 125% of the value of the home plus exaggerated income multiples. Banks have now tightened up their lending criteria considerably. Recently, The Mortgage Market review came into effect (2014) which has imposed further restrictions on banks and building society lending and requires a stringent set of checks carried out before a mortgage is approved. All lenders insist on larger minimum deposits. This will vary with the bank or building society and you should also scan the Sunday newspapers in particular for details of best buys for mortgages. Refer to chapter 4 for details on help to buy, with the government guaranteeing deposits.

Stamp duty- What is stamp duty and who pays it?
Stamp Duty — Stamp Duty Land Tax (SDLT) official jargon — is a tax you pay when you buy a home. The buyer pays stamp duty – not the person selling. Stamp duty applies to both freehold and leasehold purchases over £125,000

2. How much do I have to pay?
You usually pay Stamp Duty Land Tax (SDLT) on increasing portions of the residential property price above £125,000 when you buy residential property, for example a house or flat. There are different rules if you're buying your first home and the purchase price is £500,000 or less. You must still send an SDLT return for transactions under £125,000 unless they're exempt.

Rates on your first home
You can claim a discount (relief) so you do not pay any tax up to £300,000 and 5% on the portion from £300,001 to £500,000.

You're eligible if:

- you, and anyone else you're buying with, are first-time buyers
- you complete your purchase on or after 22 November 2017

If the price is over £500,000, you follow the rules for people who've bought a home before.

If you paid SDLT on a shared ownership property between 22 November 2017 and 29 October 2018

You can apply for a refund if you paid SDLT but you did not get relief. Write to HMRC and include:

- the Unique Transaction Reference Number (UTRN) from your SDLT return - ask your solicitor if you're not sure
- how much you overpaid
- your bank or building society account name, number and sort code

You must get your application to HMRC by 28 October 2019. You can also ask HMRC to send the refund to someone else, for example your solicitor.

Rates if you've bought a home before
Freehold sales and transfers

See table overleaf. You can also use this table to work out the SDLT for the purchase price of a lease (the 'lease premium').

*

Property or lease premium or transfer value	SDLT rate
Up to £125,000	Zero
The next £125,000 (from £125,001 to £250,000	2%
The next £675,000 (from £250,001 to £925,000	5%
The next £575,000 (the portion from £925,001 to £1.5M	10%
The remaining amount (the portion above £1.5m	12%

Example If you buy a house for £275,000, the SDLT you owe is calculated as follows:

- 0% on the first £125,000 = £0
- 2% on the next £125,000 = £2,500
- 5% on the final £25,000 = £1,250
- Total SDLT = £3,750

New leasehold sales and transfers

When you buy a new residential leasehold property you pay SDLT on the purchase price of the lease (the 'lease premium') using the rates above. If the total rent over the life the lease (known as the 'net present value') is more than £125,000, you also pay SDLT of 1% on the portion over £125,000 - unless you buy an existing ('assigned') lease.

Higher rates for additional properties

You'll usually have to pay 3% on top of the normal SDLT rates if buying a new residential property means you'll own more than one.

You may not have to pay the higher rates if you exchanged contracts before 26 November 2015.

If you're replacing your main residence

You will not pay the extra 3% SDLT if the property you're buying is replacing your main residence and that has already been sold. If there's a delay selling your main residence and it has not been sold on the day you complete your new purchase:

- you'll have to pay higher rates because you own 2 properties
- you may be able to get a refund if you sell your previous main home within 36 months

There are special rules if you own property with someone else or already own a property outside England, Wales and Northern Ireland.

Special rates

There are different SDLT rules and rate calculations for:

- corporate bodies
- people buying 6 or more residential properties in one transaction
- shared ownership properties
- multiple purchases or transfers between the same buyer and seller ('linked purchases')
- purchases that mean you own more than one property
- companies and trusts buying residential property

Other costs

A solicitor normally carries out conveyancing of property. However, it is perfectly normal for individuals to do their own conveyancing.

All the necessary paperwork can be obtained from legal stationers and it is executed on a step-by-step basis. It has to be said that solicitors are now very competitive with their charges and, for the sake of between £600-£900, it is better to let someone else do the work which allows you to concentrate on other things.

Land Registry

The Land Registry records all purchases of land in England and Wales and is open to the public (inspection of records, called a property search). The registered title to any particular piece of land or property will carry with it a description and include the name of owner, mortgage, rights over other persons land and any other rights. There is a small charge for inspection. A lot of solicitors have direct links and can carry out searches very quickly. Not all properties are registered although it is now a duty to register all transactions. (See chapter 6, conveyancing)

Energy Performance Certificates (EPC's)

EPC's are compulsory. An EPC surveyor will assess the property and looks at all the ways a house or flat can waste heat, such as inadequate loft insulation, lack of cavity wall insulation, draughts and obsolete boilers. After the assessment they will award a rating from A (as good as it gets) to G (terrible). The document also includes information and advice on how to improve matters, such as lagging the water tank or installing double-glazing. An EPC will cost between £120-130 and will be valid for ten years. Improvements made while the certificate is in force will not need a new survey. However, watch out for companies that offer them for higher prices. Always search around.

Structural surveys

The basic structural survey is the homebuyers survey and valuation which is normally carried out by the building society or other lender. This will cost you between £250-£500 and is not really an in-depth survey, merely allowing the lender to see whether they should lend or not, and how much they should lend. Sometimes, lenders keep what they refer to as a retention, which means that they will not forward the full value (less deposit) until certain defined works have been carried out. If you want to go further than a homebuyers report then you will have to instruct a firm of surveyors who have several survey types, depending on how far you want to go and how much you want to spend.

A word of caution. Many people go rushing headlong into buying a flat or house. They are usually exhilarated and wish to complete their purchase fairly quickly in order to establish their new home. If you stop and think about this, it is complete folly and can prove very expensive later. A house or flat is a commodity, like other commodities, except that it is usually a lot more expensive. A lot can be wrong with the commodity that you have purchased which is not immediately obvious. Only after you have completed the deal and paid over the odds for your purchase do you begin to regret what you have done.

The true price of a property is not what the estate agent is asking, certainly not what the seller is asking. The true market price is the difference between what a property in good condition is being sold at and your property minus cost of works to bring it up to that value. Therefore, if you have any doubts whatsoever, and if you can afford it get a detailed survey of the property you are proposing to buy and get the works required costed out. When negotiating, this survey is an essential tool in order to arrive at an accurate and fair price. Do not rest faith in others, particularly when you alone stand to lose.

One further word of caution. As stated, a lot of problems with property cannot be seen. A structural survey will highlight those. In some cases it may not be wise to proceed at all.

Mortgage fees-Mortgage indemnity insurance. This is a one-off payment if you are arranging a mortgage over 70-80% of lenders valuation. This represents insurance taken out by the lender in case the purchaser defaults on payments, in which case the lender will sell the property to reclaim the loan. It is to protect the mortgage lender not the buyer. The cost of the insurance varies depending on how much you borrow. A 90% mortgage on a £60,000 property will cost between £300-600. For a 100% mortgage it is usually much higher. You have to ask yourself, if you are paying up to £2,000 for this kind of insurance on a 100% mortgage, is it not better to try to raise the money to put down a bigger deposit. Always think about the relative economics. A lot of money is made by a lot of people in house buying and selling. The loser is usually the buyer or seller, not the host of middlemen. So think carefully about what you are doing.

Mortgage arrangement fees

Depending upon the type of mortgage you are considering you may have to pay an arrangement fee. You should budget for a minimum of £400.

Buildings insurance

When you have purchased your property you will need to take out buildings insurance. This covers the cost of rebuilding your home if it is damaged. It also covers the cost of subsidence, storm and flood damage, burst pipes and other water leaks and vandalism and third party damage generally. The insurance company will tell you more about elements covered. It is worth shopping around for buildings insurance as prices vary significantly. Many banks/building societies also supply buildings insurance if you arrange a mortgage with them. You shouldn't immediately take up their offer, as they are not always the most competitive. Websites such as www.confused.com can provide a range of quotes for you.

Removals

Unless you are not moving far and are considering doing it yourself, you should budget for hiring a removal firm. This will depend on how many possessions you have and how much time and money you have. Take care when choosing the removal firm. Choose one who comes recommended if possible. There are other costs too. Reconnection of telephone lines and possibly a deposit, carpets, curtains and plumbing-in washing machines. How much you pay will probably depend on how handy you are yourself. There are also smaller incidental costs such as redirecting mail by the post office. We will be discussing moving home in more depth later on in chapter 8.

Costs of moving

The table below will give you an idea of typical costs, such as solicitors fees, stamp duty, land registry fees and search fees when buying a property. The costs are based on a purchase of a typical London property. Other costs as discussed above will be extra. It has to be stressed that, apart from the stamp duty and Land Registry Fees (which should be checked as below is for guidance only) solicitor's costs and searches will vary. Searches will cost more in different areas and solicitors fees will come down.

House price	Solicitors fees (av)	Stamp duty	Land Registry	Search fees	Total fees
£150,000	£900	£500	200	200	1800
£200,000	£900	£1500	200	200	£2800
£300,000	£1000	5000	280	235	6,515
£500,000	£1000	15,000	280	280	16,560
£750,000	1069	27,500	280	280	29129
£1m	1372	66250	920	235	68777
£1.5m	1895	116,500	920	235	119550
£2m	2208	166,500	920	235	169863
£2.5m	2723	236500	920	235	240378
£3m	3656	260,000	920	235	264811
£3.5m	4231	310,000	920	235	315386
£4m	4871	360,000	920	235	366026

The process of buying a property

Having considered the basic elements of buying a property, the next step is to find the property you want. As we have discussed, this is a long and sometimes dispiriting process. Trudging around estate agents, sorting through mountains of literature, dealing with mountains of estate agents details, scouring the papers and walking the streets! However, most of us find the property we want at the end of the day. It is then that we can put in our offer. One useful way of determining the respective values of property in different areas is to visit a website set up for that purpose www.hometrack.co.uk. This particular site collects price information from selected estate agents in different postcode areas across the country. Before you decide to look, a little research into prices and comparisons with what you can afford might be useful.

Making an offer

You should put your offer in to the estate agent or direct to the seller, depending who you are buying from. As discussed earlier, your offer should be based on sound judgement, on what the property is worth not on your desire to secure the property at any cost. A survey will help you to arrive at a schedule of works and cost. If you cannot afford to employ a surveyor from a high street firm then you should try to enlist other help. In addition, you should take a long and careful look at the house yourself, not just a cursory glance. Look at everything and try to get an idea of the likely cost to you of rectifying defects. However, I cannot stress enough the importance of getting a detailed survey. Eventually, you will be in a position to make an offer for the property.

You should base this offer on sound judgement and you should provide a rationalisation for your offer, if it is considerably lower than the asking price. You should make it clear that your offer is subject to contract and survey (if you require further examination or wish to carry out a survey after the offer).

Putting your own home on the market

Most people moving try to secure the sale of their own home before looking for a new one. If you haven't started to sell your house yet, you are advised to do so as soon as possible. You need also to arrange finance. A lot of people have had the nightmarish experience of stepping into an estate agents and being besieged by "independent" financial advisors wishing to sell you their product. Be very careful at this stage. See "getting your mortgage" chapter 5.

Exchange of contracts

Once the buyer and seller are happy with all the details stated in the contract and your conveyancer can confirm that there are no outstanding legal queries, those conveyancing will exchange contracts. The sale is now legally binding for both parties. You should arrange the necessary insurances, buildings and contents from this moment on as you are now responsible for the property.

Buying with a friend

The 1996 Family Law Act brought in the concept of cohabiting couples having the same rights as married couples. This will apply particularly if your marriage starts to break up and you wish to ascertain property rights. However, it is wise to draw up a cohabitation contract prior to purchase which will put in writing how the property is shared and will make clear the situation after break-up. The cohabitation contract can include any conditions you wish and is drawn up usually by a solicitor. There are standard forms for cohabitation agreements which can include financial arrangements stating who pays for the mortgage, who can call for a sale, mutual wills, and who pays for and owns possessions. You can obtain a leaflet concerning this from a Citizens Advice Bureau or from a solicitor.

Completing a sale

This is the final day of the sale and normally takes place around ten days after Exchange. Exchange and completion can take place on the same day if necessary but this is unusual.

On day of completion, you are entitled to vacant possession and will receive the keys. See chapter 6 for more details on the conveyancing process.

Buying at auction

Although many people will go through the traditional route of acquiring property through an estate agent, there are other routes, one main one being the auction. Buying at auction requires a different set of skills and you need to know what you are buying, where it is and what the problems are, if any.

Why is it being sold at auction? Certainly, you need to act fairly quickly as you need to inspect the property before auction day, arrive at the final bid price that you will not exceed and be prepared to complete within 28 days.

What is a property auction?

The process is very similar to the normal method of private sale. However, for an auction sale the seller and their solicitor carry out all the necessary paperwork and legal investigations prior to the auction. Subject to the property receiving an acceptable bid, the property will be 'sold' on auction day with a legally binding exchange of contracts and a fixed completion date.

Different types of property auction houses

Auction houses vary in size and the amount of business that they conduct and the frequency with which they hold auctions. Most will sell both residential and commercial property and each will have its own style of operation, and fee structure. Large auction houses will hold auctions frequently, perhaps every two months and will have around 250 lots for sale. A lot of the auctions happen in London. Most of the large auction houses will deal with property put forward by large institutions, such as banks selling repossessions.

Also local authorities and will advertise the sales in the mainstream media and trade papers. The medium size auction houses will hold auctions as frequently as they can, in regional venues, such as racecourses and conference centres, and depending on stock, usually every two to three months, tending to advertise locally. The small auction houses will have far fewer lots and will hold their sales in smaller local venues. They may advertise in local press but more often will trade on word of mouth.

Those who attend auctions

As you might imagine, all sorts of people attend auctions. The common denominator is that they are all interested in buying property.

Property investors are most common at auction, people who are starting out building a portfolio or those who have large portfolios that they wish to expand. They tend to fall into two groups, those who are after capital appreciation, i.e. buy at a low value and build the capital value and those who are looking for rental income. Then there are the property traders who like a quick profit from buying and 'flipping' property. These types usually have intimate knowledge of an area and are well placed to make a quick profit. Then we have the developers who look for small profitable sites or larger sites where property can be built and sold on. The sites can have existing buildings on them or can be vacant lots with or without planning permission. Last, but not least, we have those people who intend to buy solely for the purpose of owner occupation, look to buy a below- value property that they can redesign and make their own.

What types of property are suitable for auction?

There is strong demand for all types of properties offered at auction. These may be properties requiring updating, those with short leases, development sites with or without planning permission, repossessions, forced sales and, investment properties. Also ground rents, probates, receivership sales and local authority properties. However, any type of property can be sold at auction and initially the property will be inspected to discuss specific criteria and the current situation. Extensive research will be carried out by the auction house and advice offered as to whether auction is the appropriate method of sale.

Why is property being sold at an auction?

There are a number of reasons why property is sold at an auction:
- A quick sale is needed, often due to the owner being in financial difficulties or it is a repossession
- There are structural problems which prevent the property being sold easily in the conventional manner.
- Properties sold by public bodies. Here you get all sort of property, including weird and wonderful properties such as public toilets and police stations, all of which may have their uses.

- The property is unique and there are no direct comparisons, such as lighthouses and the above mentioned public toilet.

It is always best to find out why exactly the property is being sold at auction. Is it so difficult to get rid of because of some inherent reason? Ask why is this property at auction and not being sold in the conventional way? Who exactly is the vendor and what if any are the problems stopping it being sold conventionally? The reasons that the property is at auction may be entirely innocent but it is always worth finding out to avoid future problems.

What happens next?
Once you have found your auction, to receive a complimentary auction catalogue you should contact the Auctioneers and this will give the information about the properties being offered for sale. You can also download a catalogue from the auctioneers website. The catalogue includes descriptions of the available properties, legal information, viewing arrangements and a guide price, which is purely an indication of a realistic selling price. This should not be taken as a firm asking or selling price and should be relied upon as a guide only. Professional advice must be taken in relation to any lot in which there is an interest.

For lots where viewings are arranged, these are carried out on a block basis and are published in all advertising and in the auction catalogue. Any prospective purchaser is welcome at these viewings and should the scheduled appointments be inconvenient, alternative arrangements can be made. Any interest must be registered with the Auctioneers in order that prospective purchasers may be kept informed as to the progress of the sale.

Bidding for a property

The lots will be offered and the bidding taken to the highest possible level and once the gavel falls, the contracts will be exchanged. The buyer purchases the property at the price they bid - this cannot be negotiated and the stipulated terms cannot be changed. The buyer will then pay 10% of the purchase price on the day and completion occur 28 days later. The funds are then paid to the seller less the fees of the Auctioneers and those of the seller's solicitor.

The atmosphere of an auction room can be extremely exciting and competitive and it is often the case that an interested party will bid in excess of the figure that had previously been set as their maximum. In some cases, the prices achieved at auction can be higher than those achieved by private treaty.

The seller will provide a legal pack that may be inspected at any time. Auctioneers will strongly advise that professional advice is obtained from a legal representative. Details of the seller's solicitors will be available and, should a mortgage be required, it is advisable to have this in place prior to the sale. Again, Auctioneers strongly advise that funding is discussed with a professional advisor prior to attending the sale.

The successful buyer will be required to pay 10% of the purchase price on the day, together with a buyer's premium which is normally £250 including VAT. The balance of the purchase price is required on the agreed completion day and this is normally 28 days after the auction, however this can vary so best to check with the auction house.

How do prospective purchasers find out legal and survey information for the properties in which they are interested?

A legal pack is requested from each of the vendor's solicitors and this contains copies of all legal papers, which will be required by any prospective purchasers for them to make an informed decision regarding the purchase of any lot. The pack will include office copy entries and plans, the relevant local authority search, leases (if applicable), Special Conditions of Sale, replies to pre-contract enquiries and any other relevant documents. A copy of these legal packs can usually be obtained from auctioneers for a small charge. Should any additional information be required, the seller's solicitors are listed in the catalogue and can be contacted directly. All legal packs are available for inspection at each auction.

Any purchase at auction takes place under the assumption that documentation and the terms of the contract have been read.

It is strongly recommended that any potential purchasers carry out full investigations for any lot in which they have an interest and a survey is an integral part of that investigation.

How is finance arranged?

Should a mortgage be required, approval in principle must be obtained prior to auction. Lenders are now familiar with the auction process and are usually willing to provide a mortgage offer for buyers intending to purchase at auction. A valuation and survey will be required along with legal evidence that there are no issues that will affect the value.

It is essential that the lender can provide funds within the timescale for completion. On the day of the auction, the purchaser will need to pay 10% of the purchase price and must ensure there are cleared funds to pay this amount. Sometimes, finance can be arranged through an Auctioneers on request.

Can lots be bought before auction?

Vendors may consider offers submitted before auction day. Any such offers need to be submitted in writing to an Auctioneers - this will be referred to the vendor and their instruction will be passed on to the prospective purchaser. Any offers will have to be unconditional and the buyer must be in a position to exchange contracts and pay the required deposit before auction day. With most auctioneers, no offers are considered within five days of the auction.

House swapping

House swapping is an unorthodox but cost effective way of obtaining the property that you are looking for. It is a very efficient way of buying a property. Essentially, you find the property that you want and the seller moves into your house. There is no chain because you are cutting out other buyers. Obviously, the biggest problem is finding someone that you want to swap with and who wants to swap with you.

In practice, the estate agent should be the ideal key player in any swap arrangement. They have a large number of people on their books and who have provided details of their requirements. However, this way of operating seems to be beyond all but the most enterprising estate agencies. In practice, most swaps happen through coincidence.

Saving money through swapping homes

There is a significant saving to be made by swapping homes. If you are the one trading down, for example you have a home worth £275,000 and you want to swap it for a flat worth £150,000, the owner of the flat will be paying for your house with part cash part property. As far as HMRC is concerned this is not a sale on which you would pay stamp duty, but a transfer on which you would pay a notional sum of just £5. However, in this particular type of transaction solicitors must draw up the deal as a single contract with the more expensive property paid partly in kind and partly in cash. You can also save on estate agents fees if you find your swap independently. A useful website dealing with home swaps is:

www.home-swap.org.uk. Registration on the site is free.

****

Chapter 4

More About Mortgages

Most people purchasing a property will need a mortgage. There are many products on the market and deposits are not always required. However, it is crucial that you are in possession of all the facts when making a decision about a mortgage.

Financial advisers will give you plenty of advice but not always the best advice. Sometimes it is better to go to the lender direct. Before you talk to lenders, work out what your priorities are, such as tax advantage, early repayment and so on. Make sure that you are aware of the costs of life cover.

Lenders-Banks and building societies

There is little or no difference between the mortgages offered by banks and building societies. Because banks borrow against the wholesale money markets, the interest rate they charge to borrowers will fluctuate (unless fixed) as and when their base rate changes. Building societies however, which will rely more heavily on their savers deposits to fund their lending, may adjust the interest rate charged for variable mortgages only once a year. This may be a benefit or disadvantage, depending on whether rates are going up or down.

Centralised lenders

Centralised lenders borrow from the money markets to fund their lending and have no need for the branch network operated by banks and building societies. Centralised lenders, which came to the fore during the 1980s, particularly the house price boom, have been criticised for being quick to implement increases but slow to implement decreases, through rate reductions. This is, simply, because they exist to make profit. Therefore, you should be cautious indeed before embarking on a mortgage with lenders of this kind.

Brokers and "independent" financial advisors

Brokers act as intermediaries between potential borrowers and mortgage providers. If they are "tied" agents they can only advise on the products of one bank, insurance company or building society. If they are independent they should, technically, advise and recommend on every product in the market place.

A word of warning. It is up to you to ask detailed questions about any product a broker offers you. Since 2013, advisors have to charge a fee and advertise this fee. prior to this they charged a commission, the costs of which fell onto the borrower. Many brokers sell unsuitable products because they receive healthy commissions. In the 1980s it became impossible to enter an estate agents without being forced to enter into discussions with financial advisers who were intent on selling you products which made them a lot of money. If possible, you should arrange a mortgage direct with a bank and avoid so called independent brokers.

How much can you borrow?

There is a standard calculation for working out the maximum mortgage that you will be allowed. For one borrower, three times annual salary, for a joint mortgage, two or two and a half times combined. Lenders, however, will vary and some will lend more. Be very careful not to overstretch yourself. As stated, banks and building societies have tightened up their lending criteria and mortgages are hard to obtain without hefty deposits. The Financial Conduct Authority have introduced tough new rules to ensure that no one can borrow more than they can afford to repay. These rules represent a further tightening up after the fiasco of the last ten years which has ultimately led to the present crisis. Under the new rules, interest only mortgages will only be offered to people with a firm and clear repayment plan, rather than simply relying on the rise in house prices to cover repayment of the capital. Lenders will also have to take account of future interest rate increases on repayment costs.

Mortgage Market Review

New rules came into force in April 2014 means that those seeking a mortgage should brace themselves for a long wait to see a mortgage adviser, three-hour interviews at the bank and forensic analysis of your daily spending habits.

Even after jumping through all those hoops, success is not guaranteed – experts have warned thousands of buyers and home owners are likely to be rejected because they do not meet the new requirements.

The City regulator, the Financial Conduct Authority (FCA), has introduced the new rules, known as the Mortgage Market Review, to ensure borrowers are issued with mortgages they can afford both now and in the future. The FCA was concerned that lenders were making it too easy to get a mortgage before the financial crisis.

Many households borrowed too much money and found they were unable to keep up their repayments when the financial crisis struck.

So-called "self-cert" loans, where borrowers declared their income but did not have to prove or "certify" it, were common and people routinely exaggerated earnings to borrow more. Interest-only loans also caused problems. Borrowers flocked to these deals because their monthly repayments were lower, but they had no way to repay the capital at the end of the loan.

To ensure safer lending in future, mortgage providers are now responsible for assessing whether customers can afford the loan in the long term. This includes buyers and those who are remortgaging and want to increase the size of the loan, vary the time frame or transfer it to a new property.

Deposits

Most banks and building societies used to lend 95% maximum, some more than that. It is now possible, if you look around, to get a high loan to valuation as there is a lot of competition with low interest rates here to stay for the moment, although as always, lenders will usually require higher deposits. The best source of information for reputable lenders is in the weekend newspapers. However, still, the more that you put down the better deal that you are likely to get from the lender.

Government Help-to-Buy Scheme
Help to Buy equity loan

You can get a low-interest loan towards your deposit. This is called an equity loan.

Eligibility

The home you buy must:

- be a new build
- have a purchase price of up to £600,000 in England (or £300,000 in Wales)
- be the only one you own
- not be sub-let or rented out after you buy it
- be one that you can show you can't afford (if you're applying in Wales)

How it works

With an equity loan:

- you need a 5% deposit
- the government will lend you up to 20% (up to 40% in London)
- you need a mortgage of up to 75% for the rest (up to 55% in London)

You must buy your home from a registered Help to Buy builder. There are different rules for equity loans in Wales.

Example

For a £200,000 property	Amount			Percentage		
Cash deposit	£10,000			5%		
Equity loan	£40,000	(£80,000	in London)	20%	(40%	in London)
Mortgage	£150,000	(£110,000	in London)	75%	(55%	in London)

Equity loan fees

You'll have to pay equity loan fees, but not for the first 5 years. In the sixth year, you'll be charged a fee of 1.75% of the loan's value. The fee then increases every year, according to the Retail Prices Index plus 1%. Your Help to Buy agent will contact you to set up these monthly fee payments. You'll also get a statement about your loan each year. Fees don't count towards paying back the loan.

Paying back the loan

You must pay back the loan after 25 years or when you sell your home - whichever comes first. The amount you pay back depends on how much your home is worth (the market value).

Example

Market value of your home	Equity loan	Amount
Bought for £200,000	20%	Borrowed £40,000
Sold for £250,000	20%	Pay back £50,000

You can pay back part or all of your loan at any time. The smallest repayment you can make is 10% of the market value of your home.

Example

Market value of your home	Percentage	Amount
Bought for £200,000	Borrowed 20%	£40,000
Value at time of payment £220,000	Paying back 10%	£22,000

Help to Buy ISA

If you're saving to buy your first home, the government will top up your savings by 25% (up to £3,000). If you're buying with someone else, they can also get a Help to Buy ISA.

You don't have to pay it back.

Eligibility

The home you buy must:

- have a purchase price of up to £250,000 (or up to £450,000 in London)
- be the only home you own
- be where you intend to live

How it works

Your first payment to your ISA can be up to £1,200 and then you can pay up to £200 each month. When you buy your property, your solicitor or conveyancer will apply for the extra 25%.

Example

Your savings	Government payment	Total
£1,600 (minimum)	£400	£2,000
£4,000	£1,000	£5,000
£12,000 (maximum)	£3,000	£15,000

How to apply

Apply to one of the following providers:

- Aldermore Bank
- Bank of Scotland
- Barclays

- Clydesdale Bank
- Halifax
- HSBC
- Lloyds Bank
- Nationwide
- NatWest
- Newcastle Building Society
- Santander
- Ulster Bank
- Virgin Money
- Yorkshire Bank

Buying through shared ownership

You can get a shared ownership home through a housing association. You buy a share of your home (between 25% and 75%) and pay rent on the rest.

There are different rules in Northern Ireland and Scotland. Contact your local authority to find out about buying a shared ownership home in Wales.

Eligibility

You can buy a home through shared ownership if your household earns £80,000 a year or less (or £90,000 a year or less in London) and any of the following apply:

- you're a first-time buyer
- you used to own a home, but can't afford to buy one now
- you're an existing shared owner

Older people

If you're aged 55 or over you can buy up to 75% of your home through the Older People's Shared Ownership (OPSO) scheme. Once you own 75% you won't pay rent on the rest.

Disabled people

You can apply for a scheme called home ownership for people with a long-term disability (HOLD) if other Help to Buy scheme properties don't meet your needs, eg you need a ground-floor property. With this scheme you can buy up to 25% of your home. If you're disabled you can also apply for the general shared ownership scheme and own up to 75% of your home.

Buying more shares

You can buy more of your home after you become the owner. This is known as 'staircasing'.The cost of your new share will depend on how much your home is worth when you want to buy the share. It will cost:

- more than your first share if property prices in your area have gone up
- less than your first share if property prices in your area have gone down

The housing association will get your property valued and let you know the cost of your new share. You'll have to pay the valuer's fee.

Selling your home

If you own a share of your home, the housing association has the right to buy it first. This is known as 'first refusal'. The housing association also has the right to find a buyer for your home. If you own 100% of your home, you can sell it yourself.

How to apply

To buy a home through a shared ownership scheme contact the Help to Buy agent in the area where you want to live. For more information go to:

www.helptobuy.gov.uk/equity-loan/find-helptobuy-agent

Joint mortgages

If you want a joint mortgage, as for any other shared loan you and your partner have a shared responsibility for ensuring that the necessary repayments are made. If something happens to one partner then the other has total responsibility for the loan.

Main types of mortgage
Endowment

With this type of mortgage, you have to take out an endowment insurance policy which is then used to pay off the mortgage loan in a lump sum at the end of the term. There are a number of different types designed to achieve the same end:

- Low cost with profits. This is the usual sort of endowment, guaranteeing to pay back part of the loan only. However, because bonuses are likely to be added, it is usually enough to pay off the loan in full;
- Unit linked endowment. With this, the monthly premiums are used to buy units in investment funds. The drawback is that there is no guarantee how much the policy will be

worth on maturity, since this depends on how well the investments have performed.

A word of warning. Endowment products were pushed heavily by financial brokers. There was an obsession with them in the 1980's. This is because they earn big commission for those people that sell them. Like a lot of salespeople, motivated by greed salespeople, some advisers failed to reveal the down side.

This is:

-Endowments are investment linked and there is no guarantee that they will have matured sufficiently at the end of the term to repay the mortgage. This leaves you in a mess. A repayment mortgage will definitely have paid off the mortgage at the end of the term. If you change your mortgage and decide that you do not wish to continue with an endowment mortgage, and so cash in the policy early you will almost certainly get a poor return unless it is close to maturity. In the early years of the policy, most of your payments will go towards administration and commission (a fact that your broker does not always reveal). The alternative in these circumstances is to maintain the endowment until it matures, treating it as a stand-alone investment which will, hopefully, make you some money eventually.

Repayment mortgages

This mortgage, where the borrower makes regular repayments to pay the mortgage off over the term is a fairly safe bet. However, if you plan to move house every five years then this will not necessarily be the best mortgage for you. With a repayment mortgage, you pay interest every month but only a small proportion of the capital, particularly in the early years of the mortgage. An endowment mortgage, while more risky, could be better for you under these circumstances, since you can transfer the plan from property to property, while it can, hopefully, grow steadily as it matures.

Pension mortgages

Similar to the other products except that the payments go into a personal pension plan with the remainder after paying the mortgage forming the basis of a pension. The same characteristics apply as to the others.

Interest only mortgage

The borrower pays interest only on the loan, and decides how he or she will pay the loan off at the end. The lender will want to know this too, particularly in the light of the new rules being introduced, mentioned above.

Mixed mortgages

A new development is that one or two lenders now allow borrowers to mix a combination of mortgages in one deal, customising the mortgage to suit each individual.

Foreign currency mortgages

Some foreign banks offer short-term mortgages in the foreign currency of that bank. Their lending criteria can be much more relaxed than trying to borrow from a British lender. The advantage of this sort of mortgage depends on currency fluctuations. If the pound is stable or rises, the borrower benefits. If the pound drops, the borrower will have to pay more. These types of home loans should be left to more sophisticated investors as there is the potential to get into trouble unless you have a clear grasp on the implications of such a mortgage.

Cashbacks

You probably saw the adverts offering large sums of cashback if you took a particular product. If you read the small print, unless you took the highest mortgage available with the highest deposit then you would not get anywhere near such a sum. This mortgage was typical of the many mortgages on offer in the pre-credit crunch times. You would be very hard pushed to see such an offer now.

Buy to Let Mortgages

Buy-to-let (BTL) mortgages are for landlords who buy property to rent it out. The rules around buy-to-let mortgages are similar to those around regular mortgages, but there are some key differences. Read on for more information about how they work, how to get one and what mistakes to avoid.

Who can get a buy-to-let mortgage?

You can get a buy-to-let mortgage if:

- You want to invest in houses or flats.
- You can afford to take a risk. Investing in property is risky, so you shouldn't take out a BTL mortgage if you can't afford to take that risk.
- You already own your own home. You'll struggle to get a

buy-to-let mortgage if you don't already own your own home, whether outright or with an outstanding mortgage.

- You have a good credit record and aren't stretched too much on your other borrowings such as your existing mortgage and credit cards.
- You earn £25,000+ a year. Otherwise you might struggle to get a lender to approve your buy-to-let mortgage.
- You're under a certain age. Lenders have upper age limits, typically between 70 or 75. This is the oldest you can be when the mortgage ends not when it starts. For example, if you are 45 when you take out a 25-year mortgage it will finish when you're 70.

How do buy-to-let mortgages work?

Buy-to-let mortgages are a lot like ordinary mortgages, but with some key differences:

- Interest rates on buy-to-let mortgages are usually higher.
- The fees also tend to be much higher.
- The minimum deposit for a buy-to-let mortgage is usually 25% of the property's value (although it can vary between 20-40%).
- Most BTL mortgages are interest-only. This means you don't pay anything each month, but at the end of the mortgage term you repay the capital in full.
- Most BTL mortgage lending is not regulated by the Financial Conduct Authority (FCA). There are exceptions, for example, if you wish to let the property to a close family member (e.g. spouse, civil partner, child, grandparent, parent or sibling).

These are often referred to as a consumer buy to let mortgages and are assessed according to the same strict affordability rules as a residential mortgage.

How much you can you borrow for buy-to-let mortgages

The maximum you can borrow is linked to the amount of rental income you expect to receive. Lenders typically need the rental income to be a 25–30% higher than your mortgage payment. To find out what your rent might be talk to local letting agents, or check the local press and online to find out how much similar properties are rented for.

Where to get a buy-to-let mortgage

Most of the big banks and some specialist lenders offer BTL mortgages. It's a good idea to talk to a mortgage broker before you take out a buy-to-let mortgage, as they will help you choose the most suitable deal for you.

Using price comparison websites

Comparison websites are a good starting point for anyone trying to find a mortgage tailored to their needs. the following are the most popular.

- Moneyfacts
- Money Saving Expert
- MoneySuperMarket
- Which?

Comparison websites won't all give you the same results, so make sure you use more than one site before making a decision.

It is also important to do some research into the type of product and features you need before making a purchase or changing supplier.

Plan for times when there's no rent coming in

Don't assume that your property will always have tenants. There will almost certainly be 'voids' when the property is unoccupied or rent isn't paid and you'll need to have a financial 'cushion' to meet your mortgage payments. When you do have rent coming in, use some of it to top up your savings account. You might also need savings for major repair bills. For example, the boiler might break down, or there may be a blocked drain.

Stamp Duty Land Tax (SDLT)for buy to let properties is an extra 3% on top of the current SDLT rate bands.

What to do if you feel that you have been given wrong advice

The mortgage lending market is very complicated and many people have suffered at the hands of financial advisors and others who have given incorrect advice. Mortgage regulation has not been very tight. However, the basic framework is as follows:

- Sales of mortgage linked investments like endowments or pensions are regulated by the Financial Conduct Authority. Anyone selling investments must be qualified and registered and must be able to clearly demonstrate that the policy that they have recommended is suitable. All registered individuals and firms are inspected by regulators and can be fined or expelled from the industry if guilty of wrongly selling products. By contrast, information on mortgages is currently regulated by the industry only, voluntarily, under a code of mortgage practice sponsored by the Council of Mortgage Lenders. Although most of the big players are signed up to the code there are still some who are not. Check first before taking advice.

How to complain

- Complain first to the company that sold you the product, going through its internal complaints procedure.
- If you are unhappy with the firm's decision, approach the relevant complaints body. For mortgage advisors employed directly by lenders, or complaints about lenders generally, contact the Financial Ombudsman Service on 0800 023 4 567 or www.financial-ombudsman.org.uk
- For mortgage lenders which are not building societies or banks but which are signed up to the mortgage code, the Chartered Institute of Arbitrators 020 7421 7455 www.ciarb.org will assist.
- If your complaint is about a mortgage broker, contact the Chartered Institute of Arbitrators which may be able to help if the firm is registered under the code.
- Complaints about endowments, pensions and other investments is handled by the Financial Conduct Authority 0800 111 67 68 www.fca..org.uk and are dealt with by the financial ombudsman Service.

The most common complaint is to do with endowments. A lot of people bought products which they came to regret. They are a major source of profit to the provider-and all those in between-but the person left holding the problem is the consumer. If you believe that you have been given bad advice about anything to do with the insurance or investment side of a product then you should approach the Financial Services Authority. The Building Society Association or the British Bankers Association have free publications that should help you. In addition, the Consumers Association, "Which" runs regular articles on mortgages. Remember - always ask questions. Never rush into anything. Always take advice if you are uncertain. Banks and building societies themselves are usually a better source, a safer source than individual advisers.

Borrowing and the internet

Almost all lenders have their own sites and many operate internet only loans with keener rates than those available on the high street. But there are also growing numbers of mortgage broker sites, offering mortgage calculators so that you can work out how much you can afford to borrow and how much the true cost of your loan will be. A list of internet sites can be found in the useful addresses and websites section at the back of this book.

****

Chapter 5

Selling Your Home

Estate agents

Ask for quotes from at least three agents before instructing one or more of them. The fee is normally based on the selling price of the house and is between 1 - 3 per cent of the final selling price. However, VAT (currently 20%) will be added on to this. The next chapter on conveyancing gives an idea of the processes involved once a buyer is found.

DIY Selling

If you want to save the cost of instructing an agent to sell your house, you could try to sell it yourself. Around 4 - 5% of homes in the UK are sold privately. There are a number of useful guides which are dedicated to this subject. One site worth visiting is www.yopa.co.uk/homeowners-hub/guide-selling-house-privately.

Setting the price if selling yourself

You need to see how much similar properties are sold for in the area. If this proves difficult, get a professional valuation. See Yellow Pages under Surveyors or Valuers or contact the Royal Institution of Chartered Surveyors. A valuation report will only value and will not assess structural soundness. A survey is needed for that. Put together the sales particulars in the same way that an estate agent would. It is advisable to put a disclaimer on these details such as "these particulars are believed to be accurate and are set out as a general outline only for the guidance of interested buyers. They do not constitute, nor constitute parts of, an offer or contract.

Advertising your property independently

There are a number of ways you can advertise your property. Local papers will advertise for you and also there are free ad papers. In addition, there are a number of companies with a computerised sales network who will charge you a flat fee for advertising. Be accurate with the details - you may leave yourself open to damages through misrepresentation. If an offer is made to you then you should then hand matters over to your solicitor. As discussed, some sellers handle their own conveyancing lock stock and barrel. This includes the legal side. However, this book cannot advise you on legal conveyancing. That is a separate matter. Suffice to say that it follows a standard format. It is easier, in the light of the reduced prices available to appoint a solicitor to do this side for you.

Selling using online agents

Online estate agents can help you sell your property without using a traditional high-street agent. Run via websites and call centres, they tend to offer a more basic service than you'd receive from a high-street agent and, as a result, they charge lower fees. Two types of online agents have emerged over the last few years. Online-only estate agents require the seller to do most of the work themselves, from taking photos and creating an advert to handling buyer enquiries, conducting viewings and negotiating offers. But many online-only estate agents have now evolved into hybrid agencies, employing 'local property experts' to handle buyer enquiries, accompany viewings and negotiate offers.

How do online estate agents work?

The services offered by online estate agents - particularly hybrid agencies - are similar to those offered by high-street agents, but often in a more stripped-back form. Most online estate agents now offer the option of valuing and marketing your home and arranging property viewings. Many can also negotiate and accept offers on your behalf, and liaise with your conveyancer, other estate agents and buyers until the sale is complete. These services usually incur a higher fee than the basic service.

While high-street estate agents will usually charge you a percentage of your property's selling price, online estate agents generally charge fixed fees. This means that using an online agent is often much cheaper, especially if your home is worth a lot of money. For example, if you sold a property worth £250,000 using a high-street estate agency that charged 1.3% commission, you'd pay £3,250. Online estate agents typically charge a flat fee of between £300 and £1,500, regardless of the value of your property.

A major downside of online estate agents' lower prices is that you'll often have to pay up front, regardless of whether they end up selling your home or not. Paying a fixed fee also reduces the agent's incentive to sell your property for the highest possible price. However, some online estate agents offer the option to pay once you've completed the sale but for a slightly higher price, reducing the risk of wasting your money. Some also offer a deferred payment option, where you pay at a defined point in the future, for example, 10 or 12 months down the line. This may involve entering into a credit agreement with the agency, so make sure you fully understand the terms before signing on the dotted line.

Property valuations

An online-only agent is likely to use online data to value your home, while hybrid online estate agents will send a 'local expert' to provide a valuation. However, you won't necessarily get a valuer with specific knowledge of the local market.

Remember you don't have to use the valuation provided. Ask three firms – high street or online – and go with an average, or whatever you think is the right price based on recent similar examples you've found through your own research. Inviting a variety of companies to value your home and talking to them about their sales process will also enable you to more deeply understand the differences between online and high street agents.

Marketeting

Online estate agents will list your home on their site as well as other online property portals such as Rightmove and Zoopla. Some will install a 'for sale' sign outside your house, although they might charge extra for this. High street estate agents will do all of the above as a standard part of their service, and can also place adverts in their branch windows.

Viewings

The default option with most online estate agents is that you conduct the viewings yourself. However, a lot of online agents now offer accompanied viewings for an extra fee of around £300, or as part of a more expensive package than their standard offering.

Buyer vetting

Some (though not all) online estate agents will vet buyers, typically getting details of names, finances and whether potential buyers are already part of a chain.

Communicate with an online agent

Someone will visit to take photographs and create floor plans if you sign up for this option, and you'll meet the 'local property expert' if the agency sends one round. However, all other contact will usually be via email or phone - and many online estate agencies offer online portals where you can access helplines or chat services outside traditional working hours, with some offering 24/7 support.

Rights when using an online estate agent

Online estate agents are governed by the same regulations that cover high street estate agents.As with high street agents, online estate agents must be members of a government-approved redress scheme – the Property Ombudsman Limited or the Property Redress Scheme. Your agent has to be clear about which redress scheme they are a member of, and the scheme should be your first port of call if you have a problem.Trading Standards will also investigate agents that it believes have acted in breach of the 1979 Estate Agent Act, which sets out minimum standards of conduct for estate agents.

Pros and cons of online estate agents

Online estate agents can be a great money-saving option when you're selling your house, but you should be aware of the pros and cons of these services before making a decision.

Pros of using an online estate agent:

- Fees: in most cases, using an online estate agent will be a lot cheaper than using a high-street agent. The more expensive your home is, the more you stand to save if they charge a flat fee.
- Convenience: it can sometimes be easier to get hold of online estate agents. Their call centres are open during evenings and weekends, so they are able to deal with queries outside of working hours (although some high-street agents offer this, too).
- Flexibility: packages can be tailored to your specific requirements, and you can often track viewings and feedback online (some high-street agents also offer this).
- Freedom to use multiple agents: generally, there is no contract period, which means you can instruct other estate agents if you wish.

Cons of using an online estate agent
- Lack of local knowledge: even online agents with regional reps could struggle to compete with a high-street agent who knows your neighbourhood and its property market inside out.
- Legwork: some online estate agents won't negotiate offers or act as a middleman to progress your sale to completion. Having to manage communications with buyers and solicitors on your own can be time-consuming and stressful.
- Viewings: you usually have to conduct viewings yourself, so you'll need to be comfortable showing strangers around your home and be available during evenings and weekends.
- Paying up front: if you opt for this type of package, you won't be paying on results. In fact, you'll have to pay even if that

company doesn't end up selling your house.

- Selling price: because most online estate agents charge a flat fee rather than commission, they have less incentive to get the best price for you. That said, they have reputations to maintain, and many companies claim they usually achieve the asking price.

Selling at Auction

Advantages of auction

In chapter 3, we looked at buying properties at auction. Here are a few tips for you when selling a property at auction. An auction is an efficient and cost effective way of selling property and if prepared properly with intensive marketing, advertising and mailing, will result in the greatest possible exposure of the lots offered. To maximize the effectiveness of the marketing, considerable thought must be given to the guide price, which needs to be tailored to generate competitive bidding in the auction room, thus ensuring that the best price is being achieved. Although some properties are more suitable for sale by private treaty, taking this route does present uncertainties over terms such as sale price and timing of exchange and completion.

Selling by auction however, offers a high degree of certainty that a sale will be achieved on a given day and, significantly, on the fall of the gavel an immediate binding contract is formed. As no further negotiation is permitted the entire sale process, from instruction to exchange of contracts can be, is achieved within as little as six to eight weeks. For vendors with a large number of properties to sell, auctions provide a highly efficient method of sale allowing for a total or phased disposal programme selling in individual lots thus maximising receipts. For those selling in a fiduciary capacity, there is the added advantage of the sale being entirely open and transparent. Most types of property are suitable for auction provided that a realistic reserve price is agreed.

Quick Results

The entire process, from instruction to exchange of contracts, can be achieved within as little as six to eight weeks.

****

Chapter 6

Conveyancing a Property

Conveyancing, or the practice of conveyancing, is about how to transfer the ownership of land and property from one person or organisation to another. Land and property can include freehold property, leasehold property (residential) or can include business leases. *Essentially, the process of conveyancing lays down clear procedures for the conveyancer and also sets out each party's position during the sale or acquisition.*

Most conveyancing, in particular relatively simple residential transactions, is carried out electronically, with the Land Registry aiming to move towards a complete digital process in the next few years. Before understanding the process of conveyancing, however, it is essential to understand something about the legal forms of ownership of property.

Legal ownership of property

There are two main forms of legal ownership of property in Great Britain. If you are about to embark on the sale or acquisition of a house or flat (or business) then you will be dealing in the main with either freehold or leasehold property.

It is very rare indeed to find other forms of ownership, although the government has introduced a form of ownership called 'common hold' that in essence creates the freehold ownership of flats, with common responsibility for communal areas.

Freehold property

In general, if you own the freehold of a house or a piece of land, then you will be the outright owner with no fixed period of time and no one else to answer to (with the exception of statutory authorities).

There may be registered restrictions on title, which will be discussed later. The property will probably be subject to a mortgage so the only other overriding interest will be that of the bank or the building society. The responsibility for repairs and maintenance and general upkeep will be the freeholders. The law can intervene if certain standards are not maintained. The deed to your house will be known as the "freehold transfer document" which will contain any rights and obligations. Usually, the transfer document will list any "encumbrances" (restrictions) on the use of the land, such as rights of way of other parties, sales restrictions etc. The deeds to your home are the most important documentation. As we will see later, without deeds and historical data, such as the root of title, it can be rather complicated selling property. This is why the system of land registration in use in this country has greatly simplified property transactions.

Any person owning freehold property is free to create another interest in land, such as a lease or a weekly or monthly tenancy, subject to any restrictions the transfer may contain.

Leasehold property

If a person lives in a property owned by someone else and has an agreement for a period of time, usually a long period, over 21 years and up to 99 years or 125 years, in some cases 999 years, then they are a leaseholder.

The conveyancing of leasehold property is, potentially, far more problematic than freehold property, particularly when the flat is in a block with a number of units. The lease is a contract between landlord and tenant which lays down the rights and obligations of both parties and should be read thoroughly by both the leaseholder and, in particular, the conveyancer. Once signed then the purchaser is bound by all the clauses in the contract. It is worth taking a little time looking at the nature of a lease before discussing the rather more complex process of conveyancing. Again, it has to be stated that it is of the utmost importance that both the purchaser and the vendor understand the nature of a lease.

The lease-Preamble

The start of a lease is called the preamble. This defines the landlord and purchaser and also the nature of the property in question (the demise). It will also detail the remaining period of the lease.

Leaseholders covenants

Covenants are best understood as obligations and responsibilities. Leaseholder's covenants are therefore a list of things that leaseholders should do, such as pay their service charges and keep the interior of the dwelling in good repair and not to, for example, alter the structure. The landlord's covenants will set out the obligations of the landlord, which is usually to maintain the structure and exterior of the block, light common parts etc.

One unifying theme of all leasehold property is that, notwithstanding the landlord's responsibilities, it is the leaseholder who will pay for everything out of a service charge.

Leases will make detailed provisions for the setting, managing and charging of service charges, which should include a section on accounting. All landlords of leaseholders are accountable under the Landlord and Tenant Act 1985, as amended. These Acts will regulate the way a landlord treats a leaseholder in the charging and accounting of service charges.

In addition, the 1996 Housing Act, as amended by the 2002 Commonhold and Leasehold Reform Act has provided further legislation protecting leaseholders by introducing the right of leaseholders to go to Firs Tier Tribunals if they are unhappy with levels and management of charges and also to carry out audits of charges. It is vital that, when buying a leasehold property that you read the lease. Leases tend to be different from each other and nothing can be assumed. When you buy a property, ensure that the person selling has paid all debts and has contributed to some form of "sinking fund" whereby provision has been built up for major repairs in the future. Make sure that you will not be landed with big bills after moving in and that, if you are, there is money to deal with them. After a lease has been signed then there is little or no recourse to recoup any money owed.

These are all the finer points of leases and the conveyancer has to be very vigilant. In particular read the schedules to the lease as these sometimes contain rather more detail.

One of the main differences between leasehold and freehold property is that the lease is a long tenancy agreement which contains provisions which give the landlord rather a lot of power to manage (or mismanage) and it is always a (remote) possibility that a leaseholder can be forced to give up his or her home in the event of non-compliance with the terms of the lease. This is known as forfeiture.

Under legislation referred to earlier, a new 'no fault right to manage' has been introduced. This enables leaseholders who are unhappy with the management of their property, to take over the management with relative ease. The Act applies to most landlords, with the exception of Local Authorities. These powers go a long way to curb the excesses or inefficiencies of numerous landlords and provide more control and greater security for leaseholders.

Check points

There are key areas of a lease that should be checked when purchasing. Some have already been discussed.

- What is the term left on the lease?
- Is the preamble clear, i.e. is the area which details landlord, tenant and demised (sold) premises, clear?
- Is the lease assignable- i.e. can you pass on the lease without landlords permission or does it need surrendering at sale or a license to assign?
- What is the ground rent and how frequently will you pay it?
- What is the level of service charge, if any, and how is it collected, apportioned, managed and accounted for?
- What are the general restrictions in the lease, can you have pets for example, can you park cars and do you have a designated space?
- What are the respective repairing obligations? As we have seen, the leaseholder will pay anyway but the landlord and leaseholder will hold respective responsibilities. This is an important point because occasionally, there is no stated responsibility for upkeep and the environment deteriorates as a consequence, diminishing the value of the property.

Two systems of conveyancing

After gaining an understanding of the nature of the interest in land that you are buying, it is absolutely essential to understand the two systems of conveyancing property in existence, as this will determine, not so much the procedure because the initial basic steps in conveyancing, such as carrying out searches, are common to both forms of land, registered and unregistered, but the way you go about the process and the final registration are different.

Registered and unregistered land

In England and Wales the method of conveyancing to be used in each particular transaction very much depends on whether the land is *registered* or *unregistered* land. If the title, or proof of ownership, of land and property has been registered under the Land Registration Acts 1925-86 then the Land Registry (see below) will be able to furnish the would-be conveyancer with such documentation as is required to establish ownership, third party rights etc. If the land has not been registered then proof of ownership of the land in question must be traced through the title deeds.

Registered land

As more and more conveyancing is falling within the remit of the Land Registry, because it is compulsory to register land throughout England and Wales, it is worth outlining this system briefly at this stage. The Land Registration Acts of 1925 established the Land Registry (HM Land Registry). The Land Registry is a department of the Civil Service, at its head is the Chief Land Registrar. All applications to the Land Registry must be made within the district in question.

There is a specific terminology in use within conveyancing, particularly within the land registry:

a) *a piece of land*, or parcel of land is known as a *registered title*
b) the owner of land is referred to as the *registered proprietor*
c) a conveyance of registered land is called *a transfer*
d) a transaction involving registered land is known as *a dealing*

The main difference between the two types of conveyancing *registered* and *unregistered* concerns what is known *as proof of title*. In the case of land that is unregistered the owner will prove title by showing the would-be purchaser the documentary evidence which shows how he or she came to own the land and property.

In the case of registered land the owner has to show simply that he or she is registered at the Land Registry as the registered proprietor. Proof of registration is proof of ownership, which is unequivocal. In registered land the documents proving ownership are replaced by the fact of registration. Each separate title or ownership of land has a title number, which the Land Registry uses to trace ownership, or confirm ownership. The description of each title on the register is identified by the *title number,* described by reference to the filed plan (indicating limits and extent of ownership). With registered conveyancing the Land Registry keeps the register of title and file plan and title. The owner (proprietor) is issued with a Land Certificate. If the land in question is subject to a mortgage then the mortgagee is issued with a Land Certificate.

Production of the Land Certificate

With registered land, whenever there is a sale, or disposition, then the Land Certificate must be produced to the Land Registry in the appropriate district. If proved that a Certificate is lost or destroyed then a new one can be issued by the Land Registry.

The key steps in the process of conveyancing property

Before the buyer exchanges contracts on a property, whether registered or unregistered, and then completes the purchase a number of searches are always carried out. These are:

Enquiry's before contract
Local land charges search
Enquiry's of the local authority
Index map search

Making enquiry's before contract

These are enquiry's to the seller, or the Vendor of the property and are aimed at revealing certain facts about the property that the seller has no legal obligation to disclose to the buyer. There are certain matters, which are always raised. These are:

a) Whether there are any existing boundary disputes
b) What services are supplied to the property, whether electricity, gas or other
c) Any easements or covenants in the lease. These are stipulations in the lease, which give other certain rights, such as rights of way.
d) Any guarantees in existence

Planning considerations
a) Adverse rights affecting the property
b) Any fixtures and fittings

c) Whether there has been any breach of restriction affecting the property

If the property is newly built, information will be required concerning any outstanding works or future guarantees of remedying defects. Where a property is leasehold, information will be required about the lessor.

Registered conveyancers will use a standard form to raise these enquiry's, so that the initial search is exhaustive. As part of the move towards openness in the process of buying and selling property, and also an attempt to speed up the process of sale, the Law Society has introduced new forms which the solicitor, or buyer if carrying out his or her own conveyancing, is being encouraged to use. These are Seller's Property Information Forms relating to freehold and leasehold property, that the seller and solicitor will respectively fill in, a form relating to fixtures, fittings and contents and a form relating to complete information and requisitions on title. These forms can be obtained from a legal stationers, and have the pre-fix Prop 1-7.

If a conveyancer is being used then it is advisable to ask whether or not they are using these newly introduced forms. The main point is that you should think long and hard about the type of questions that should be raised. The vendor does not have to answer the questions, but beware a vendor who refuses to disclose answers. Answers given by the vendor do not form part of the subsequent contract and therefore cannot be used against that person in the event of future problems. However, the Misrepresentations Act of 1976 could be evoked if a deliberate misrepresentation has caused problems.

Local land charges search

The Local Land Charges Act 1975 requires District Councils, London Borough Councils and the City of London Corporation to maintain a Local Land Charges Registry for the area.

Local land charges can be divided into two areas:

a) Financial charges on the land for work carried out by the local authority
b) restrictions on the use of land

The register is further divided into twelve parts:
a) general financial charges
b) specific financial charges
c) planning charges
d) miscellaneous charges and provisions
e) charges for improvements of ways over fenland
f) land compensation charges
g) new town charges
h) civil aviation charges
i) open cast coal mining charges
j) listed buildings charges
k) light obstruction notices
l) drainage scheme charges

All charges are enforceable by the local authority except g and i, which are enforced by statutory bodies and private individuals generally. A buyer should search in all parts of this particular register and this can be done by a personal or official search. A personal search, as the name suggests, involves the individual or their agent attending at the local authority office and, on paying the relevant fee, personally searching the register. The charges are registered against the land concerned and not against the owner. The official search is the one most favored because, in the event of missing a vital piece of information the chances of compensation are far higher than with a personal search.

With the official search a requisition for a search and for an official certificate of search is sent to the Registrar of Local Land Charges for the area within which the land is situated. There is a fee and the search is carried out by the Registrars staff, which results in a certificate being sent to the person making the request, which clearly outlines any charges. The Registrar may require a plan of the land as well as the postal address. Separate searches are made of each parcel of land being purchased.

Local authority searches

There is a standard form in use for these particular types of searches. This is known as "Con 29 England and Wales" Revised July 2016, with the format of the form differing slightly for inner London boroughs. Any of the forms in the process can be obtained from legal stationers.

The standard forms in use contain a statement to the effect that the local authority is not responsible for errors unless negligence is proved. Many of the enquiries relate specifically to planning matters, whilst other elements of the search are concerned about roads and whether they are adopted and whether there are likely to be any costs falling onto property owners.

We will be considering planning matters concerning the

individual property a little later. Other enquiry's relate to possible construction of new roads which may affect the property, the location of sewers and pipes and whether the property is in an area of compulsory registration of title, a smoke control area or slum clearance area. The form used is so constructed that part 2 of the form contains questions, which must be initialled by the purchaser before they are answered. Again these questions cover planning and other matters.

Other enquiry's can be asked by the individual, which are answered at the authorities discretion. In addition to the above, which are the major searches, there are others that the conveyancer has to be aware of. These are as follows:

Searches in the Index map and parcels index of the Land register

If the land has been registered the title will be disclosed and whether it is registered leasehold or freehold. Registered rent charges are also disclosed by the search. (See chapter 7.)

Commons Registration Act (1965) search

This act imposes a duty on County Councils to keep a register relating to village greens and common land and interests over them, such as right of way.

Coal mining search

The request for this search if relevant, is designed to reveal the whereabouts of mineshafts and should be sent to the local Area Coal Board office, or its equivalent. The search will disclose past workings and any subsidence, proposed future workings and the proximity of opencast workings. It is usually well known if there is a problem, or potential problem with coal mining in an area and this search is essential if that is the case.

Other enquiry's

There are a number of other bodies from which it might be appropriate to request a search. These include British Rail, statutory undertakers such as electricity and gas boards, planning authorities generally, rent assessment committees and so on. These will only usually be necessary if there is a direct link between the property being purchased and a particular circumstance within an area or property.

Planning matters relating to specific properties

It is obviously very necessary to determine whether or not any illegal alterations have been carried out to the property you wish to purchase, before reaching the point of exchange of contracts. This is to ensure that the vendor has complied with relevant planning legislation, if any material changes have been made, and that you will not be required at a later date to carry out remedial work. The Local Authority maintains a register of planning applications relating to properties within their boundaries. In addition, the register will also reveal any planning enforcement notices in force against a particular property.

Questions such as these, and also any questions relating to the effect of Structure or Local plans, (specific plans relating to local and borough wide plans for the future) should be made in writing to the local authority or an individual search can be carried out. Usually they are carried out if there is any suspicion that planning regulations may have been breached.

In addition, there may be other considerations, such as whether the building is listed or whether tree preservation orders relating to trees within the cartilage of the property are in force. It is certainly essential to know about these. It is highly recommended that all of these searches are carried out and completed before contracts are exchanged.

The contract for sale

As with many other transactions, a sale of land is effected through a contract. However, a contract, which deals with the sale of land, is governed by the requirements of the Law of Property (miscellaneous provisions) Act 1989, the equitable doctrine of specific performance and the duty of the vendor to provide title to the property.

The Law of Property Act (Miscellaneous provisions) 1988 provides that contracts dealing with the sale of land after 26th September 1989 must be in writing. The contract must contain all the terms and agreements to which the respective parties to the transaction have agreed. The provisions of the Act do not apply to sales at a public auction, contracts to grant a short lease and contracts regulated under the Financial Services Act 1986. If the person purchasing is doing so through an agent then the agent must have authority to act on behalf of the purchaser. Examples of agents are auctioneers and solicitors, also estate agents. If the phrase "subject to contract" is used in a sale then the intention of both parties to the contract is that neither are contractually bound until a formal contract has been agreed by the parties, signed and exchanged.

Therefore, the words "subject to contract" are a protective

device, although it is not good to depend on the use of these words throughout a transaction

Procedures in the formation of contract

The vendor's solicitor will usually draw up an initial contract of sale. This is because only this person has access to all the necessary initial documents to begin to effect a contract. The draft contract is prepared in two parts and sent to the purchaser's solicitor (if using a solicitor), the other side will approve or amend the contract as necessary. Both sides must agree to any proposed amendments. After agreement has been reached, the vendor's solicitor will retain one copy of the contract and send the other copy to the solicitor or person acting for the other side. The next stage is for the vendors solicitor to engross (sign and formalise) the contract in two parts. Both parts are then sent to the purchaser's solicitor or other agent who checks that they are correct then sends one part back to the vendor's solicitor.

The Contents of a contract

A contract will be in two parts, *the particulars of sale* and the *conditions of sale*. The particulars of sale give a physical description of the land and also of the interest, which is being sold. A property must be described accurately and a plan may be attached to the contract to emphasize or illustrate what is in the contract. The particulars will also outline whether the property is freehold or leasehold and what kind of lease the vendor is assigning, i.e., head lease (where vendor is owner of the freehold) or underlease, where the vendor is not.

It is very important to determine what kind of lease it is that is being assigned, indeed whether it is assignable or whether permission is needed from the landlord and it is recommended that a solicitor handle this transaction. This is because any purchaser of a lease can find his or her interest jeopardized by the nature of the lease. Where a sub-lease, or under lease is being purchased, the purchasers interest can be forfeited by the actions of the head lessee, the actions of this person being out of control of the purchaser.

Rights, such as easements and also restrictive covenants, which are for the benefit of the land, should be expressly referred to in the particulars of sale. In addition, the vendor should refer to any latent defects affecting his or her property, if known. This includes any encumbrances, which may affect the property.

Misdescription

If the property in the particulars of sale is described wrongly, i.e. there is a mis-statement of fact, such as describing leasehold as freehold land, calling an under-lease a lease or leaving out something that misleads the buyer, in other words, if the misdescription is material, then the purchaser is entitled to rescind the contract. Essentially the contract must describe what is being sold and if it does not, and the buyer is mislead then the contract is inaccurate. If the misdescription is immaterial and insubstantial, and there has been no misrepresentation then the purchaser cannot rescind the contract. However, if the misdescription has affected the purchase price of the property then the purchaser can insist on a reduction in the asking price. The purchaser should claim this compensation before completion takes place. The vendor has no right to rescind the contract if the misdescription is in the purchaser's favour, for example, the area of land sold is greater than that intended. Neither can the vendor compel the purchaser to pay an increased purchase price

Misrepresentation

Misrepresentation is an untrue statement of fact made by one party or his or her agent, which induces the other party to enter into the contract. An opinion and a statement of intention must be distinguished from a statement of fact.

There are three types of misrepresentation, fraudulent misrepresentation, negligent misrepresentation and innocent misrepresentation.

Fraudulent misrepresentation is a false statement made knowingly or without belief in its truth, or recklessly. The innocent party may sue through the tort of negligence either before or after the contract is complete and rescind the contract. Negligent misrepresentation, although not fraudulent, is where the vendor or his or her agents cannot prove that the statement they made in relation to the contract was correct. Remedies available are damages or rescission of the contract. Innocent misrepresentation is where the statement made was neither fraudulently or negligently but is still an untrue statement. Rescission is available for this particular type of misrepresentation. Rescission of contract generally is available under the Misrepresentation Act 1967 s 2(2).

Non-disclosure

Generally, in the law of contract, there is the principle of "caveat emptor" "let the buyer beware". In other words, it is up to the purchaser to ensure that what he or she is buying is worth the money paid for it. Earlier we talked about the importance of searches and also, particularly, the importance of the structural survey. Although the vendor has some responsibility to reveal any defects in the property it is always very advisable for the purchaser to ensure that all checks prior to purchase are carried out thoroughly.

Signing the contract

The vendors solicitor will obtain the vendors signature to the contract, when he is satisfied that the vendor can sell what he is purporting to do through the contract. The purchaser's solicitor or agent will do the same, having checked the replies to all enquiry's before contract. It is also essential to check that a mortgage offer has been made and accepted.

Exchanging contracts

Neither party to the sale is legally bound until there has been an exchange of contracts. At one time, a face to face exchange would have taken place. However, with the rapid increases in property transactions this rarely happen nowadays. Exchange by post is more common. The purchaser will post his or her part of the contract together with the appropriate cheque to cover the agreed deposit, to the purchaser's solicitor or person acting on behalf of that Person. The purchaser's solicitor will usually insert the agreed completion date. On receiving this part of the contract the vendor will add his or her part and send this off in exchange. At this stage, both parties become bound under the contract.

A contract to convey or create an estate in land is registrable as a class C (IV) land charge, an estate contract. You should take further advice on this, as it is not current practice to do so.

Completion

The requirements concerning completion are detailed thoroughly in the general conditions of sale. Payment on completion is one such detail. Payment on completion should be by one of the following methods:

a) legal tender;

b) bankers draft;

c) an unconditional authority to release any deposit by the stakeholder

d) any other method agreed with the vendor.

At common law, completion takes place whenever the vendor wishes and payment is to be made by legal tender. Also dealt with in the general conditions is failure to complete and notices to complete. Failure to complete can cause difficulty for one of the other parties and the aggrieved party can serve notice on the other to complete by a specific date. The notice has the effect of making "time of the essence" which means that a specific date is attached to completion, after which the contract is discharged. It is worth mentioning here that it is very advisable indeed to be aware of scams that have been taking place which have cost purchasers dear. This is a sophisticated email scam. Fraudsters are intercepting emails between homebuyers, sellers and their solicitors to target the large sums of money that are exchanged in property transactions. The criminals hijack or spoof the client or solicitors email accounts and provide a bank account into which they instruct funds to be sent. they then drain the money as soon as possible. It can then be very difficult for the purchaser to get the money back.

In the light of this, if you are involved in selling or buying a property, at the point of making any transaction, you should contact the actual firm itself, if necessary going down to see them, to check that all bank account details are correct.

It is always advisable to instruct a solicitor in your home town so that you can readily go to see them if necessary.

Return of pre-contract deposits

The vendor must return any deposit paid to the purchaser if the purchaser drops out before the exchange of contracts. This cannot be prevented and was the subject of a House of Lords ruling.

The position of the parties after exchange of contracts

Once a contract has been exchanged, the purchaser is the beneficial owner of the property, with the vendor owning the property on trust for the purchaser. The vendor is entitled to any rents or other profits from the land during this period, has the right to retain the property until final payments have been made and has a lien (charge/right) over the property in respect of any unpaid purchase monies. The vendor is bound to take reasonable care of the property and should not let the property fall into disrepair or other damages to be caused during the period between exchange and completion. If completion does not take place at the allotted time and the fault is the purchasers then interest can be charged on the money due.

The purchaser, as beneficial owner of the property is entitled to any increase in the value of the land and buildings but not profits arising. The purchaser has a right of lien over the property, the same as the vendor, in respect of any part of the purchase price paid prior to completion.

Bankruptcy of the vendor

In the unfortunate event of the vendor going bankrupt in between exchange and completion, the normal principles of bankruptcy apply so that the trustee in bankruptcy steps in to the vendor's shoes. The purchaser can be compelled to complete the sale. The trustee in bankruptcy is obliged to complete the sale if the purchaser tenders the purchase money on the completion day.

Bankruptcy of the purchaser

When a purchaser is declared bankrupt in between sale and completion all of his or her property vests in the trustee in bankruptcy. In these circumstances, the vendor can keep any deposit due to him.

Death of Vendor or purchaser

The personal representatives of a deceased vendor can compel the purchaser to sell. The money is conveyed to those representatives who will hold the money in accordance with the terms of any will or in accordance with the rules relating to intestacy if there is no will.

The same position applies to the purchaser's representatives, who can be compelled by the vendor to complete the purchase and who can hold money on the purchaser's behalf.

****

Chapter 7

Planning Moving Arrangements

At this stage, you will either have sold your home and /or be ready to move into a new one. The process of moving home is closely linked with the completion of the purchase of another home. That is, assuming that you are moving to another bought property. Of course, you may be moving to a rented home. However you choose to time your move, there are certain core tasks, as follows:

- Finalise removal and storage arrangements
- Contact electricity/gas/phone/cable companies and any other relevant company to tell them your moving date
- Organise your funds so that you can transfer all remaining money needed to complete the sale into your solicitors account for him/her to pay the sellers solicitor

One main question is: do you get a removal firm or do you do it yourself?

DIY moves
This is cheaper than hiring a removal company, especially if you have a few possessions or no big items of furniture. You will also need willing and able friends. However, do not take the decision to move yourself lightly. Think carefully about the amount of furniture that you have and the fact that your house may be a particularly difficult site to move from.

Using professionals

Professionals know what they are doing and can leave you to organise all the other aspects of moving whilst they do the donkey work. This may cost you more money. However, it may be well worth it. Use a firm which is a member of the British Association of Removers (www.bar.co.uk). Members of this body have to adhere to a code of professional practice, meet minimum standards and provide emergency service and finance guarantees.

Removers can offer various levels of packing services. The most expensive option is for the remover to pack everything. The second most expensive option is for them to pack the breakable things such as glass. The cheapest way is for the removers to provide crates and for you to do your own packing.

If you are going for the professional option:

- Get two or three estimates. You can find the names of local firms through the British Association of Removers or through the local press. There are a growing number of websites that include quotes from removal firms (see below for one of the main ones)
- You should expect estimators to go through your whole property including gardens and loft
- Check whether your possessions will be covered by your household insurance policy and extend the cover if they are not.
- Don't wait to exchange contracts to organise removers.

The following Website may be useful:

www.reallymoving.com

This site was launched in 1999 and is the leading provider of online removal services. Registering on the site will get you three quotes from removers. It also covers solicitors, surveyors and others involved in the buying and selling process.

Contacting utilities

A boring but essential task is to contact all of the companies that provide you with services to tell them that you have moved. This should be done after you exchange contracts, obtaining meter readings etc. Most utilities will ask you for confirmation of your new address and moving date in writing. If you cannot face this task then use the following website:

www.iammoving.com

This site was started in 1999 by a consortium of investors and industry figures. The claim is to be the UK's first free online change of address service. You register, enter your old and new address, supply account numbers and meter readings where relevant and iammoving will send the information to the appropriate companies. The process is quick and relatively uncomplicated.

****

Chapter 8

Buying and Selling in Scotland

Scotland has it own system of law, and buying and selling a house or flat is quite a different process from doing so in England, Wales or Northern Ireland. The system generally works more quickly and there is less risk of gazumping.

Looking for property

Solicitors, property centres and offices. These are the largest source of properties available in Scotland. Often found in town centres, the property centres provide information in a similar way to estate agents outside Scotland. Of course there are the large websites such as Rightmove and Zoopla.

Newspapers.

Daily Scottish newspapers are a good source of property. Regional and local newspapers carry many details on a regular basis.

Estate agents. These offer the same service

Home reports in Scotland

When you're buying a home in Scotland the seller will need to provide any potential buyers with a home report on their property. The only exceptions are new-builds and buildings that have recently been converted into residential properties. The home report consists of a single survey, an energy report and a property questionnaire.

The single survey contains a valuation and an assessment of the property's condition (including the roof, external walls and plumbing). You may want to consider getting a more detailed building survey done if the property is older or of a non-standard construction.

The energy report will give the property an energy efficiency rating and assess its environmental impact by looking at carbon dioxide emissions.

Completed by the seller, the property questionnaire will contain details such as whether the property has ever flooded or been treated for wood rot, as well as useful pieces of information such as what the parking arrangements are and which council tax band the home falls into.

Making an offer on a Scottish property

Properties in Scotland are usually marketed and sold by solicitors, rather than estate agents. They are either advertised at a fixed price or for 'offers around' or 'offers over' a certain price. When a property is advertised for 'offers around' or 'offers over', a closing date will be set and prospective purchasers will need to submit sealed bids before that date.

Your solicitor (see below) will work with you to prepare your offer and pass it on to the seller's solicitor on your behalf. As well as how much you're willing to pay for the property, your offer should include a proposed 'date of entry' – i.e. when you'll pay and get the keys - and other terms and conditions relating to the purchase.

Once the offers are in, the seller will then choose the offer they want to accept. No money is paid at this stage unless it's a new-build property, in which case a deposit may be required.

Conveyancing for buyers in Scotland

When buying a home in Scotland you'll need to instruct a solicitor very early on in the process. Once you've seen a property you're interested in buying, your solicitor should:

- Explain the home report to you
- Check that any alterations have been made with the necessary planning permission and building control approval
- Put together your offer with you
- Submit your offer to the seller's solicitor

Once the offers are in, the seller will choose the offer they want to accept. This doesn't have to be the highest.

If your bid is successful, your solicitor will confirm your mortgage with the lender, agree an entry date and deal with legal enquiries about the property.

Concluding the missives

They will also agree the contract with the seller's solicitor. This is known as 'concluding the missives', and it's legally binding for both the seller and buyer. At this point, the solicitor will undertake the conveyancing process to transfer the ownership of the property.

Settlement

On the date of entry that's agreed in the contract, you'll pay the whole of the purchase price in exchange for the keys to the property. This point is known as 'settlement'. Your solicitor will pay any <u>LBTT</u> (see below) that is due, register the change of ownership with the Registers of Scotland, and lodge title deeds with your mortgage lender (you'll get a copy too).

Land and Buildings Transaction Tax

Land and Buildings Transaction Tax (LBTT) is the Scottish equivalent of stamp duty and is charged on the following:

- First-time buyers: properties costing £175,000+
- Home movers: properties costing £145,000+
- Buy-to-let or second home buyers: properties costing £40,000+

Buying a tenement property

Technically speaking, a tenement is a building or part of a building containing two or more flats that are separated horizontally and designed to have separate ownership.

This includes houses converted into flats, high-rise blocks, and both traditional and modern buildings. Tenements can also be office blocks, although most are residential.

More than a quarter of the housing in Scotland consists of tenements. If you're buying a flat in a tenement property, you will own your flat and a share of the tenement's common parts, and a share of the land upon which the tenement is built. The title deeds to each flat should set out who owns what. If the deeds don't do this, certain rules will apply - for example, the owner of the top-floor flat will own the roof space above it. Talk to your solicitor to find out how it works for the property you're buying. It's important that you fully understand the setup.

Tenement maintenance costs

As a tenement flat owner you're liable for a share of maintenance costs to common parts of the tenement. Unless the repairs are essential, a majority of the flat owners must agree on whether they are needed, which can cause difficulties and delays.

What is a 'factor'?

Sometimes the titles provide for the appointment of a 'factor'. This is a person or firm with the responsibility of managing and instructing repairs. If this isn't covered in the titles, the tenement owners may agree to appoint one. Assuming the factor acts properly, the owners of all the flats will be liable for the costs of repairs.

Restrictions of use

In Scotland, most property titles have conditions that restrict their use. For example, there will usually be a condition specifying that a property won't be used for commercial gains. When a property is passed to a new owner, so too are these conditions. Your solicitor will inform you of all title conditions involved with the property you're buying, normally prior to the date of entry but after the contract is concluded. If you're unhappy with any of the title conditions, you can try asking the seller to try getting the conditions changed. However, this rarely happens and the title conditions must usually be accepted for the deal to go ahead.

Feuhold properties and feu duty

This complex system was abolished for most properties in November 2004, but check with your solicitor to make sure it doesn't apply to your property.

Joint ownership of a Scottish property

If you want to buy a home with someone else, you have two options: joint ownership or common property. It's worth talking to your solicitor about what will work best for your situation before making a decision.

Joint ownership

If you've bought a house under joint ownership and one of you dies, your share will automatically pass to the other person without any conveyancing expense. Joint owners can sell or give away their share during their lifetime, but they can't give it away in a will.

Common property

If a home is owned as 'common property', the owners can sell or give away their share during their lifetime or in a will. This can be problematic if, for example, a couple has bought the property and then splits up. Your solicitor should explain all the consequences of these clauses before you decide to use one.

Help to Buy (Scotland)

This government scheme enables people to buy new-build homes with a deposit of 5%, government equity loan of 15% and mortgage of 80%. Help to Buy is currently set to run until March 2021 in Scotland.

How the Scottish property system differs from the rest of the UK

The property-buying process in Scotland is generally quicker and less likely to fall through than it can be in the rest of the UK, excluding Northern Ireland. In fact, research found that, in 2018, 10.4% of transactions fell through in Scotland after an offer had been accepted, compared to 21.8% in England, 22.9% in Wales, and 9.6% in Northern Ireland. There are a number of reasons for this:

- Preparing a home report costs money, therefore it's more likely that the vendor is serious about selling
- The home report means that buyers are better informed about a property's condition and value at the point of making an offer, so there's less potential for them to back out later
- Gazumping - when another buyer makes a higher offer after yours has been accepted - is rare because properties are usually withdrawn from the market once a price has been agreed. Solicitors are also not allowed to continue to represent a seller if they choose to go with a different buyer, meaning they don't encourage the practice.

It will generally take four to eight weeks to buy a property in Scotland, while it's more likely to take eight to 12 weeks in England, Northern Ireland or Wales.

Chapter 9

Buying Overseas

Thousands of Britons have purchased properties overseas. However, this can be problematic and certainly basic advice is needed relating to the particular country where you are buying. There are a few general tips when buying abroad:

- Buy through a qualified and licensed agent. In most countries including France, Spain, Portugal and the USA, agents legally have to be licensed and using an unlicensed agent means that there is no comeback if things go wrong.
- Do not sign anything until you are sure that you understand it. Note that estate agents in the above countries will tend to do more of the legal work than in Britain and hence charge more commission.
- Always hire a solicitor (English speaking if you are not fluent in the local language) to act for you. In some countries, the locals do not use solicitors but you should insist. The solicitor will check that the seller owns the property and that there are no debts attached to it and that planning regulations have been met. Local searches are not as regulated as they are in the UK and it's often a case of making informal enquiries at the local town hall.
- Understand the role played by the state notary (notaire in France, notario in Spain) he or she is a state official, whose only

role is to see that the sale is completed. He or she will not act for you or the seller.

There are a number of useful websites where more information can be gained:

www.french-property-news.com

This site is the online arm of the magazine French Property News. It claims to have the most comprehensive list of properties on the web and also has details of other organisations.

www.french-property.com

For property in Spain, try www.homeespana.co.uk which specialises in all types of property includingretirement property.

For property in Eastern Europe you should go to www.eurobrix.com

Other useful websites:
For the USA-
www.primelocation.com
www.propertyshowrooms.com
www.escape2usa.co.uk

Property overseas generally
www.property-abroad.com

There are many other websites dealing with buying and selling property in most countries of the world. It goes without saying that you should learn as much about a country as possible and deal with professionals only before taking the plunge overseas.

Chapter 10

Letting a Property-Sourcing Suitable Tenants and Managing Property

Chapters 10 to 17 deal with renting out a property. Whether you have decided to rent out your property instead of selling, in the short term, or whether you are either a landlord or a would - be landlord, there are many crucial areas to be aware of when renting, not least the safety aspects, the legal aspects and the tax considerations. We will start by looking at the role of lettings agents in sourcing tenants.

Letting Agents
An amendment to the Enterprise and Regulatory Reform Act 2013 enabled the Government to require agents to sign up to a redress scheme. The Redress Scheme for Lettings Agency Work and Property Management Work (Requirement to Belong to a Scheme etc) (England) Order 2014 made membership of a scheme a legal requirement with effect from 1 October 2014. The Government also amended the Consumer Rights Act 2015 to require letting agents to publish a full tariff of their fees. (it should be noted that, from June 1st 2019, lettings agents are banned from charging tenants fees for letting a property. In addition, deposits are now capped at five weeks rent. For full details of what fees are now banned and for

deposit restrictions go to:
www.gov.uk/government/publications/tenant-fees-act-2019-guidance).

If you intend to use an agent to manage your properties then ensure that it is signed up to a redress scheme. One such scheme is The Property Ombudsman Scheme. www.tpos.co.uk.

Online lettings agents

As with online state agents, the rise of online lettings agents has been rapid and they now account for 3.5% of the market. The attractions are obvious, the costs. One of the biggest online property agents, EasyProperty.com offers 'pick and mix' services ranging from £10 a week for adverts on Right Move, Prime Location and Zoopla to 3% commission for full property management. For tenant finding with all the frills, such as hosted viewings and professional photos to check-in the total bill would be £445. This equates to less than half the commission charged by high-street agents. Another agent, Purplebricks.com is also very competitive. However, there can be drawbacks.

The main drawback is accessibility. If you have your contract with a local agent, they will be there when you want them. Online tends to be one step removed. You are strongly advised to consider what it is you want before entering into any deal with an online agent. If you do appoint an agent to manage a property you should agree at the outset, in writing, exactly what constitutes management. Failure to understand the deal can cost you dearly.

For example, in a lot of cases, an agent will charge you a fixed fee, sometimes 1 months rental, for finding a tenant, but will then exercise the right that they have given themselves in the initial contract to sign a new agreement and charge another months rent after the tenancy has expired. In this way they will charge you a months rent every six months for doing nothing at all.

What agents do

Agents will typically look after the following:

1   Transfer the utility bills and the council tax into the name of the tenant. Sign agreements and take up references.

2   Paying for repairs, although an agent will only normally do this if rent is being paid directly to them and they can make appropriate deductions.

3   Chase rent arrears.

4   Serve notices of intent to seek possession if the landlord instructs them to do so. An agent cannot commence court proceedings except through a solicitor.

5   Visit the property at regular intervals and check that the tenants are not causing any damage.

6   Deal with neighbour complaints.

7   Banking rental receipts if the landlord is abroad

8   Dealing with housing benefit departments if necessary. The extent to which agents actually do any or all of the above really depends on the caliber of the agent. It also depends on the type of agreement you have with the agent. Like your initial business plan, you should be very clear about what it is you want from the agent and how much they charge.

Beware! There are many so-called rental agencies which have popped up since the growth of the rental market. These agents are not professional, do not know a thing about property management, are shady and should be avoided like the plague. Shop around and seek a reputable agent. A typical management fee might be 10-15 percent of the rent, although there is lots of competition and lower prices can be obtained.

Advertisements

If you decide to dispense with the use of an agent, the classified advertisement section of local papers is a good place to seek potential tenants. Local papers are obviously cheaper than the nationals such as the Evening Standard in London or the broadsheets such as the Guardian. The type of newspaper you advertise in will largely reflect what type of customer you are looking for. An advert in the pages of the Times would indicate that you are looking for a well-heeled professional and this would be reflected in the type of property that you have to let. There are many free ad papers and also you may want to go to student halls of residence or hospitals in order to attract a potential tenant. When you do advertise, you should indicate clearly the type of property, in what area, what is required, i.e., male or female only, and the rent. You should try and avoid abbreviations as this causes confusion.

One consideration if looking for a tenant yourself, following the passage of the Immigration Act 2014, and the Immigration Act 2016 there is a responsibility on landlords to vet their tenants, or prospective tenants to check to see if they have a right to be in the country (The Right to Rent). More information can be obtained from www.gov.uk.

Letting your property through The public sector

One other source of income is the local authority or housing association. Quite often, your property will be taken off your hands under a five-year contract and you will receive a rental income paid direct for this period, with agreed increases. However, the local authority or housing association will demand a high standard before taking the property off your hands. Quite often the rent achieved will be lower than a comparable market rent, in return for full management and secure income.

If you wish to try this avenue then you should contact your local authority or nearest large association.

Company lets

Where the tenant is a company rather than an individual, the tenancy agreement will be similar to an assured shorthold but will not be bound by the six-month rule (see further on for details of assured shorthold tenancies). Company lets can be from any length of time, from a week to several years, or as long as you like.

The major difference between contracts and standard assured shorthold agreements is that the contract will be tailored to individual needs, and the agreement is bound by the provisions of contract law. Company tenancies are bound by the provisions of contract law and not by the Housing Acts. Note: if you are considering letting to a company you must use a letting agent or solicitor. Most companies will insist on it. The advantages of a landlord letting to a company are:

- A company or embassy has no security of tenure and therefore cannot be a sitting tenant.

- A company cannot seek to reduce the rent by statutory interventions.
- Rental payments are often made quarterly or six monthly in advance.
- The financial status of a company is usually more secure than that of an individual.
- Company tenants often require long-term lets to accommodate staff relocating on contracts of between one and five years.

The main disadvantages of company lets are:
- A company tenancy can only be to a bona fide company or embassy, not to a private individual.
- A tenancy to a partnership would not count as a company let and may have some security of tenure.
- If the tenant is a foreign government, the diplomatic status of the occupant must be ascertained, as the courts cannot enforce breaches of contract with somebody who possesses diplomatic immunity.
- A tenancy to a foreign company not registered in the UK may prove time consuming and costly if it becomes necessary to pursue claims for unpaid rent or damage through foreign courts.

Short-lets

Although company lets can be of any length, it is becoming increasingly popular for companies to rent flats from private landlords on short-lets. A short-let is any let of less than six months. But here, it is essential to check the rules with any borough concerned. Some boroughs will not allow lets for less than three months, as they do not want to encourage transient people in the neighborhood.

Generally speaking, short-lets are only applicable in large cities where there is a substantial shifting population. Business executives on temporary relocation, actors and others involved in television production or film work, contract workers and visiting academics are examples of people who might require a short-let.

From a landlord's point of view, short-lets are an excellent idea if you have to vacate your own home for seven or eight months, say, and do not want to leave it empty.

Short-let tenants provide useful extra income as well as keeping an eye on the place. Or if you are buying a new property and have not yet sold the old one, it can make good business sense to let it to a short-let tenant.

Short-let tenants are, usually, from a landlord's point of view, excellent blue-chip occupants. They are busy professionals, high earners, out all day and used to high standards. As the rent is paid by the company there is no worry for the landlord on this score either.

A major plus of short-lets is that they command between 20-50 percent more rent than the optimum market rent for that type of property. The one downside of short-lets is that no agency can guarantee permanent occupancy.

Student lets

Many mainstream letting agencies will not consider students and a lot of landlords similarly are not keen. There is the perception that students will not look after a home and tend to live a lifestyle guaranteed to increase the wear and tear on a property. However, if handled correctly, student lets can be profitable and a number of specialist companies have grown up which concentrate solely on students. Although students quite often want property for only eight or nine months, agencies that deal with students make them sign for a whole year. Rent is guaranteed by confirmation that the student is a genuine student with references from parents, who act as guarantors.

There can be a lot of money made from student lets. However, the tenancy will require more avid policing because of the nature of student lifestyle.

The DSS and housing benefit

Very few letting agencies or landlords will touch DSS or housing benefit tenants. However, as with student lets, there is another side of the coin. Quite often it is essential for a tenant on HB to have a guarantor, usually a homeowner, before signing a tenancy. Then it is up to the machinations of the benefit system to ensure that the landlord receives rent. The rent is assessed by a benefit officer, with the rent usually estimated at market price. There are rent levels set for each are that the benefit officer will not go above.

A deposit is paid normally and rent is paid direct to the landlord. This will require the tenant's consent No other conditions should be accepted by a private landlord. Rent certainly should not be paid direct to the tenant.

Although tenants on HB have a bad name, due to stereotyping, there are many reasons why a person may be on benefit and if housing benefit tenancies are managed well, then this can be a useful source of tenant.

Holiday lets

Before the Housing Act 1988 became law, many landlords advertised their properties as holiday lets to bypass the then rules regarding security of tenure. Strictly speaking, a holiday let is a property let for no more than a month to any one tenant. If the same tenant renews for another month then the landlord is breaking the law. Nowadays, holiday lets must be just that; let for a genuine holiday. If you have a flat or cottage that you wish to let for holiday purposes, whether or not you live in it yourself for part of the year, you are entering into a quite different agreement with the tenant. Holiday lets are not covered by the Housing Act. The contract is finalised by exchange of letters with the tenant where they place a deposit and the owner confirms the booking. If the let is not for a genuine holiday you may have problems in evicting the tenant.

Generally speaking, certain services must be provided for the let to be deemed a holiday let. Cleaning services and changes of bed linen are essential. The amount paid by the holiday-maker will usually include utilities but would exclude use of the telephone, fax machine etc.

If you have a property that you think is suitable for holiday let or wish to invest in one, there are numerous companies who will put you on to their books. However, standards are high and there are a certain number of criteria to be met, such as safety checks, before they will consider taking you on. If possible, you should talk to someone with some experience of this type of let before entering into an agreement with an agency. The usual problems may arise, such as ensuring occupancy all year round and the maintenance of your property, which will be higher due to a high turnover. In addition to the above, the tax situation is changing for those with holiday lets which will mean the loss of certain allowances and the tightening up of others. This is discussed further in chapter 17.

Letting through Airbnb

Over the last few years, landlords have increasingly turned to companies like Airbnb to let their properties. What started out as a good concept has, as usual been ruined by those looking for a quick return, Airbnb started out as a web based company offering an alternative to hotels, particularly in the overpriced capitals of the world. Landlords now see that there is a profit to be made by allowing a succession of short term tenants to stay in their properties. However, problems have arisen and the courts have found that for landlords with leasehold property to allow their properties to be used by a succession of short term tenants is actually a breach of the lease.

Anyone wishing to let their properties out through companies such as Airbnb should seek advice from their lender, look at their insurance, inform the neighbors and, in London be aware that if you intend to short let your property for more than 90 days you will need planning permission.

Showing the property to the tenant

Once you have found a tenant, the next stage is to make arrangements for viewing the property. It is a good idea to make all appointments on the same day in order to avoid wasting time. If you decide on a likely tenant, it is wise to take up references yourself if you are not using an agency who will do this for you. This will normally be a previous landlord's reference and also a bank reference plus a personal reference. Only when these have been received and you have established that the person(s) is/are safe should you go ahead. Make sure that no keys have been handed over until the payment has been cleared and you are in receipt of a month's rent and a month's deposit.

Deposits-Tenancy Deposit Protection Scheme

The Tenancy Deposit Protection Scheme was introduced to protect all deposits paid to landlords after 6th April 2007. After this date, landlords and/or agents must use a government authorised scheme to protect deposits. The need for such a scheme has arisen because of the historical problem with deposits. As stated, from 1st June 2019 landlords in England will be limited to 5 weeks' deposit for new and renewed tenancies (or 6 weeks if the annual rent is £50,000 or more). In addition, holding deposits are capped at one weeks rent. The scheme works as follows:

Moving into a property

At the beginning of a new tenancy agreement, the tenant will pay a deposit to the landlord or agent as usual. Within 30 days the landlord is required to give the tenant details of how the deposit is going to be protected including:

- the address of the rented property

- how much deposit you've paid

- how the deposit is protected

- the name and contact details of the tenancy deposit

125

protection (TDP) scheme and its dispute resolution service

- their (or the letting agency's) name and contact details

- the name and contact details of any third party that's paid the deposit

- why they would keep some or all of the deposit

- how to apply to get the deposit back

- what to do if you can't get hold of the landlord at the end of the tenancy

- what to do if there's a dispute over the deposit

There are three tenancy deposit schemes that a landlord can opt for:

My Deposits
www.mydeposits.co.uk
info@mydeposits.co.uk
0333 321 9401

The Tenancy Deposit Scheme
www.tenancydepositscheme.com
0300 037 1000

The Deposit Protection Service
www.depositprotection.com
0330 303 0030

The schemes above fall into two categories, insurance based schemes and custodial schemes.

Custodial Scheme

- The tenant pays the deposit to the landlord
- The landlord pays the deposit into the scheme
- Within 14 days of receiving the deposit, the landlord must give the tenant prescribed information
- A the end of the tenancy, if the landlord and tenant have agreed how much of the deposit is to be returned, they will tell the scheme which returns the deposit, divided in the way agreed by the parties.
- If there is a dispute, the scheme will hold the disputed amount until the dispute resolution service or courts decide what is fair
- The interest accrued by deposits in the scheme will be used to pay for the running of the scheme and any surplus will be used to offer interest to the tenant, or landlord if the tenant isn't entitled to it.

Insurance based schemes

- The tenant pays the deposit to the landlord
- The landlord retains the deposit and pays a premium to the insurer (this is the key difference between the two schemes)
- Within 14 days of receiving a deposit the landlord must give the tenant prescribed information.
- At the end of the tenancy if the landlord and tenant agree how the deposit is to be divided or otherwise then the landlord will return the amount agreed

- If there is a dispute, the landlord must hand over the disputed amount to the scheme for safekeeping until the dispute is resolved
- If for any reason the landlord fails to comply, the insurance arrangements will ensure the return of the deposit to the tenant if they are entitled to it.

If a landlord or agent hasn't protected a deposit with one of the above then the tenant can apply to the local county court for an order for the landlord either to protect the deposit or repay it.

Rental guarantees
The landlord is always advised to obtain a guarantor if there is any potential uncertainty as to payment of rent. One example is where the tenant is on benefits. The guarantor will be expected to assume responsibility for the rent if the tenant ceases to pay at any time during the term of the tenancy.

****

Chapter 11

What Should Be Provided Under the Tenancy?

When you let a property, you have the choice of letting it furnished or unfurnished. There is a market for both but most properties will at least have white goods installed.

Furniture

A landlords decision whether or not to furnish property will depend on the sort of tenant that he is aiming to find. The actual legal distinction between a furnished property and an unfurnished property has faded into insignificance. If a landlord does let a property as furnished then the following would be the absolute minimum:

- Seating, such as a sofa and an armchair.
- Cabinet or sideboard.
- Kitchen tables and chairs.
- Cooker and refrigerator.
- Bedroom furniture.

Even unfurnished lets, however, are expected to come complete with a basic standard of furniture, particularly carpets and kitchen goods. If the landlord does supply electrical equipment then he or she will be responsible for carrying out annual checks along with annual checks on the boiler.

Services

Service charges, and the paying of these charges, will be the responsibility of the leaseholder.

At the end of the tenancy

The tenancy agreement will normally spell out the obligations of the tenant at the end of the term. Essentially, the tenant will have an obligation to:

- Have kept the interior clean and tidy and in a good state of repair and decoration.
- Have not caused any damage.
- Have replaced anything that they have broken.
- Replace or pay for the repair of anything that they have damaged.
- Pay for the laundering of the linen.
- Pay for any other laundering.
- Put anything that they have moved or removed back to how it was.

Sometimes a tenancy agreement will include for the tenants paying for anything that is soiled at their own expense, although sensible wear and tear is allowed for. The landlord will normally be able to recover any loss from the deposit that the tenant has given on entering the premises (see previous chapter for details of the Deposit Protection Schemes). However, sometimes, the tenants will withhold rent for the last month in order to recoup their deposit. The introduction of the Deposit Protection Schemes have made this more difficult in practice. It is up to the landlord to negotiate reimbursement for any damage caused, but this should be within reason. There is a remedy, which can be pursued in the small claims court if the tenants refuse to pay but this is rarely successful.

A word on inventories

The Tenancy Deposit Scheme, has released new guidance on inventory reports to support landlords and letting agents ahead of the introduction of the Tenant Fees Act in June 2019.

Also known as the Tenant Fee Ban, the new law – which will apply to letting agents in England – means tenants cannot be charged for a number of extra services, including the provision of inventories. Landlords might then have to cover this cost themselves, rather than the charging or splitting costs with tenants. Without this option, some letting agents may choose to take the service in-house to minimise costs.

****

Chapter 12

Knowing The Law

Explaining the law

Having travelled this far in finding a property and signed up the tenant, it is now time to understand a little more about the law. Purchasing a property is one thing but the ongoing management is a different ball game altogether and requires a wide knowledge base.

As a landlord or potential landlord it is very important to understand the rights and obligations of both yourself and your tenant, exactly what can and what cannot be done once the tenancy agreement has been signed and the tenant has moved into the property.

Some landlords think they can do exactly as they please, because the property belongs to them. Tenants often do not know any differently and therefore the landlord can, and often does, get away with breaking the law. However, if you are about to embark upon a career as a landlord then it is important that you have a grasp of the key principles of the law. In order to fully understand the law we should begin by looking at the main types of relationship between people and their homes.

The freehold and the lease

In law, there are two main types of ownership and occupation of property. These are: freehold and leasehold. These arrangements are very old indeed.

Freehold

If a person owns their property outright (usually with a mortgage) then they will be a freeholder.

The only claims to ownership over and above their own might be those of the building society or the bank, which lent them the money to buy the place. They will re-possess the property if the mortgage payments are not kept up with. In certain situations though, the local authority (council) for an area can affect a person's right to do what they please with their home even if they are a freeholder. This will occur when planning powers are exercised, for example, in order to prevent the carrying out of alterations without consent.

The local authority for your area has many powers and we will be referring to these regularly in each chapter of this guide.

Leasehold

If a person lives in a property owned by someone else and has a written agreement allowing them to occupy the flat or house for a period of time i.e., giving them permission to live in that property, then they will, in the main, have a lease and either be a leaseholder or a tenant of a landlord.

The main principle of a lease is that a person has been given permission by someone else to live in his or her property for a period of time. The person giving permission could be either the freeholder or another leaseholder.

The tenancy agreement is one type of lease. If you have issued a tenancy agreement then you will have given permission to a person to live in your property for a period of time.

The position of the tenant

The tenant will usually have an agreement for a shorter period of time than the typical leaseholder. Whereas the leaseholder will, for example, have an agreement for ninety-nine years, the tenant will have an agreement, which either runs from week to week or month to month (periodic tenancy) or is for a fixed term, for example, six months. These arrangements are the most common types of agreement between the private landlord and tenant, with the six month assured shorthold being the usual tenancy offered by private landlords. See appendix for a sample tenancy agreement and notices.

The assured tenant

all tenancies, with the exceptions detailed, entered into after 15th January 1989, are known as assured tenancies. An **assured shorthold tenancy**, which is the most common form of tenancy used by the landlord nowadays, is one type of assured tenancy, and is for a fixed term of six months minimum and can be brought to an end with two months notice by serving a section 21 (of the Housing Act 1988) notice.

Assured tenancies are governed by the 1988 Housing Act, as amended by the 1996 Housing Act. It is to these Acts, or outlines of the Acts that the landlord must refer when intending to sign a tenancy and let a residential property. For a tenancy to be assured, three conditions must be fulfilled:

1. The premises must be a dwelling house. This basically means any premises, which can be lived in. Business premises will normally fall outside this interpretation.

2. There must exist a particular relationship between landlord and tenant. In other words there must exist a tenancy agreement. For example, a licence to occupy, as in the case of students, or accommodation occupied as a result of work, cannot be seen as a tenancy. Following on from this, the accommodation must be let as a single unit. The tenant, who must be an individual, must normally be able to sleep, cook and eat in the accommodation. Sharing of bathroom facilities will not prevent a tenancy being an assured tenancy but shared cooking or other facilities, such as a living room, will.

3. The third requirement for an assured tenancy is that the tenant must occupy the dwelling as his or her only or principal home. In situations involving joint tenants at least one of them must occupy.

Tenancies that are not assured

A tenancy agreement will not be assured if one of the following conditions applies:

- The tenancy or the contract was entered into before 15th January 1989.
- If no rent is payable or if only a low rent amounting to less than two thirds of the present ratable value of the property is payable.
- If the premises are let for business purposes or for mixed residential and business purposes.
- If part of the dwelling house is licensed for the sale of liquor for consumption on the premises. This does not include the publican who lets out a flat.
- If the dwelling house is let with more than two acres of agricultural land.

- If the dwelling house is part of an agricultural holding and is occupied in relation to carrying out work on the holding.
- If the premises are let by a specified institution to students, i.e., halls of residence.
- If the premises are let for the purpose of a holiday.
- Where there is a resident landlord, e.g., in the case where the landlord has let one of his rooms but continues to live in the house.
- If the landlord is the Crown (the monarchy) or a government department. Certain lettings by the Crown are capable of being assured, such as some lettings by the Crown Estate Commissioners.
- If the landlord is a local authority, a fully mutual housing association (this is where you have to be a shareholder to be a tenant) of a newly created Housing Action Trust or any similar body listed in the 1988 Housing Act.
- If the letting is transitional such as a tenancy continuing in its original form until phased out, such as a protected tenancy under the 1977 Rent Act.
- Secure tenancy granted before 15th January 1989, e.g., from a local authority or housing association. These tenancies are governed by the 1985 Housing Act).

The Assured Shorthold tenancy

The assured shorthold tenancy as we have seen, is the most common form of tenancy used in the private sector. The main principle of the assured shorthold tenancy is that it is issued for a period of six months minimum and can be brought to an end by the landlord serving two months notice on the tenant. At the end of the six-month period the tenant, if given two months prior notice, by the landlord serving a section 21 notice (see appendix) must leave.

The section 21 notice, so called because it arises out of Section 21 of the 1988 Housing Act, is the pro-forma that all landlords must use when ending a tenancy.

Any property let on an assured tenancy can be let on an assured shorthold, providing the following conditions are met:

- The tenancy must be for a fixed term of not less than six months.
- The agreement cannot contain powers, which enable the landlord to end the tenancy before six months. This does not include the right of the landlord to enforce the grounds for possession, which will be approximately the same as those for the assured tenancy (see below).
- A notice requiring possession at the end of the term is usually served two months before that date.
- A notice must be served before any rent increase giving one month's clear notice and providing details of the rent increase.

Getting possession of your property before the end of the tenancy

If the landlord wishes to get possession of his/her property, in this case before the expiry of the contractual term, the landlord has to gain a court order.

A notice of seeking possession must be served, giving fourteen days notice and following similar grounds of possession as an assured tenancy (see below). The landlord cannot simply tell a tenant to leave before the end of the agreed term

Tenancy running on after fixed term

An assured shorthold tenancy will become periodic (will run from week to week) when the initial term of six months has elapsed and the landlord has not brought the tenancy to an end. If the tenancy runs on after the end of the fixed term then the landlord can regain possession by giving the required two months notice, as mentioned above. At the end of the term for which the assured shorthold tenancy has been granted, the landlord has an automatic right to possession.

Joint tenancies: the position of two or more people who have a tenancy agreement for one property

Although it is the normal state of affairs for a tenancy agreement to be granted to one person, this is not always the case.

A tenancy can also be granted to two or more people and is then known as a joint tenancy. The position of joint tenants is exactly the same as that of single tenants. In other words, there is still one tenancy even though it is shared.

Each tenant is responsible for paying the rent and observing the terms and conditions of the tenancy agreement. No one joint tenant can prevent another joint tenant's access to the premises. If one of the joint tenants dies then his or her interest will automatically pass to the remaining joint tenants. A joint tenant cannot dispose of his or her interest in a will.

If one joint tenant, however, serves a notice to quit (notice to leave the property) on another joint tenant(s) then the tenancy will come to an end and the landlord can apply to court for a possession order, if the remaining tenant does not leave. The position of a wife or husband in relation to joint tenancies is rather more complex because the married person has more rights when it comes to the home than the single person.

Remember, the position of a tenant who has signed a joint tenancy agreement is exactly the same as that of the single tenant. If one person leaves, the other(s) have the responsibilities of the tenancy. If one person leaves without paying his share of the rent then the other tenants will have to pay instead.

Evicting assured shorthold tenants

As discussed, it is possible to gain possession of a property before the end of the fixed term if the tenancy has been seriously breached. See the chapter on regaining possession of a property. Assured shorthold tenants can be evicted only on certain grounds some discretionary, some mandatory (see below). In order for the landlord of an assured shorthold tenant to regain possession of the property, using grounds for possession such as non-payment of rent, a notice of seeking possession (of property) must be served, giving fourteen days notice of expiry and stating the ground for possession. Following the fourteen days a court order must be obtained. Although gaining a court order is not complicated, a solicitor will usually be used. Court costs can be awarded against the tenant.

Security of tenure: The ways in which a tenant can lose their home as an assured (shorthold) tenant

There are a number of circumstances called grounds (mandatory and discretionary) whereby a landlord can start a court action to evict a tenant.

The following are the mandatory grounds (where the judge must give the landlord possession) and discretionary grounds (where the judge does not have to give the landlord possession) on which a court can order possession if the home is subject to an assured tenancy.

The mandatory grounds for possession

There are eight mandatory grounds for possession, which, if proved, leave the court with no choice but to make an order for possession. It is very important that you understand these.

- *Ground One* is used where the landlord has served a notice, no later than at the beginning of the tenancy, warning the tenant that this ground may be used against him/her.
  This ground is used where the landlord wishes to recover the property as his or her principal (first and only) home or the spouse's (wife's or husbands) principal home. The ground is not available to a person who bought the premises for gain (profit) whilst they were occupied.
- *Ground Two* is available where the property is subject to a mortgage and if the landlord does not pay the mortgage, could lose the home.
- *Grounds Three and Four* relate to holiday lettings.
- *Ground Five* is a special one, applicable to ministers of religion.
- *Ground Six* relates to the demolition or reconstruction of the property.
- *Ground Seven* applies if a tenant dies and in his will leaves the tenancy to someone else: but the landlord must start proceedings against the new tenant within a year of the death if he wants to evict the new tenant.

140

- *Ground Eight* concerns rent arrears. This ground applies if, both at the date of the serving of the notice seeking possession and at the date of the hearing of the action, the rent is at least 8 weeks in arrears or two months in arrears. This is the main ground used by landlords when rent is not being paid.

One of the advantages of a court order is that you will have details of the tenant's employers and can get an attachment of earnings against the tenant.

The discretionary grounds for possession of a property

As we have seen, the discretionary grounds for possession are those in relation to which the court has some powers over whether or not the landlord can evict. In other words, the final decision is left to the judge. Often the judge will prefer to grant a suspended order first, unless the circumstances are dramatic.

- *Ground Nine* applies when suitable alternative accommodation is available or will be when the possession order takes effect. As we have seen, if the landlord wishes to obtain possession of his or her property in order to use it for other purposes then suitable alternative accommodation has to be provided.
- *Ground Ten* deals with rent arrears as does ground eleven. These grounds are distinct from the mandatory grounds, as there does not have to be a fixed arrear in terms of time scale, e.g., 8 weeks. The judge, therefore, has some choice as to whether or not to evict. In practice, this ground will not be relevant to managers of assured shorthold tenancies.
- *Ground Twelve* concerns any broken obligation of the tenancy. As we have seen with the protected tenancy, there are a number of

conditions of the tenancy agreement, such as the requirement not to racially or sexually harass a neighbour. Ground Twelve will be used if these conditions are broken.

- *Ground Thirteen* deals with the deterioration of the dwelling as a result of a tenant's neglect. This is connected with the structure of the property and is the same as for a protected tenancy. It puts the responsibility on the tenant to look after the premises.
- *Ground Fourteen* concerns nuisance, annoyance and illegal or immoral use. This is where a tenant or anyone connected with the tenant has caused a nuisance to neighbours.
- *Ground Fourteen A* this ground deals with domestic violence.
- *Ground Fifteen* concerns the condition of the furniture and neglect.

The description of the grounds above is intended as a guide only. For a fuller description please refer to the 1988 Housing Act, section 7, Schedule two,) as amended by the 1996 Housing Act) which is available at reference libraries.

As we have discussed, it is usual for the landlord of an assured shorthold tenancy to serve a notice requiring possession on the tenant giving two months notice. It is unusual for a landlord to take an assured shorthold tenant to court on one of the grounds for possession. However, these circumstances do arise, where a tenant has breached the tenancy very early on and the landlord cannot wait for the fixed term to expire.

Fast track possession

In November 1993, following changes to the County Court Rules, a facility was introduced which enables landlords of tenants with assured shorthold tenancies to apply for possession of their property without the usual time delay involved in waiting for a court date and attendance at court. This is known as "fast track possession" It cannot be used for rent arrears or other grounds. It is used to gain possession of a property when the fixed term of six months or more has come to an end, a valid section 21 notice has been served and the tenant will not move.

The contract between landlord and tenant

Typically, any tenancy agreement will show the name and address of the landlord and will state the names of the tenant(s). The type of tenancy agreement that is signed should be clearly indicated. In the main, the agreement will be an assured shorthold tenancy. The date the tenancy began and the duration (fixed term or periodic) plus the amount of rent payable should be clearly shown along with who is responsible for any other charges, such as water rates, council tax etc, and a description of the property you are renting out.

In addition to the rent that must be paid there should be a clear indication of when a rent increase can be expected. This information is sometimes shown in other conditions of tenancy, which should be given to the tenant when they move into their home. The conditions of tenancy will set out landlords and tenants rights and obligations.

If services are provided, i.e., if a service charge is payable, this should be indicated in the agreement. The tenancy agreement should indicate clearly the address to which notices on the landlord can be served by the tenant, for example, because of repair problems or notice of leaving the property. The landlord has a legal requirement to indicate this.

The tenancy agreement will either be a basic document with the above information or will be more comprehensive. Either way, there will be a section beginning "the tenant agrees." Here the tenant will agree to move into the property, pay rent, use the property as an only home, not cause a nuisance to others, take responsibility for certain internal repairs, not sublet the property, i.e., create another tenancy, and various other things depending on the property. There should also be another section "the landlord agrees". Here, the landlord is contracting with the tenant to allow quiet enjoyment of the property. The landlord's repairing responsibilities are also usually outlined.

Finally, there should be a section entitled "ending the tenancy" which will outline the ways in which landlord and tenant can end the agreement. It is in this section that the landlord should make reference to the "grounds for possession". Grounds for possession are circumstances where the landlord will apply to court for possession of his/her property. Some of these grounds relate to what is in the tenancy, i.e., the responsibility to pay rent and to not cause a nuisance.

Other grounds do not relate to the contents of the tenancy directly, but more to the law governing that particular tenancy. The grounds for possession are very important, as they are used in any court case brought against the tenant. Unfortunately, they are not always indicated in the tenancy agreement. As they are so important they are summarized later on in this chapter.

Other types of agreement
In addition to the assured shorthold tenancy agreements there are other types of agreement sometimes used in privately rented

144

property. One of these is the company let, as we discussed earlier, and another is the license agreement. The person signing such an agreement is called a licensee. Licenses will only apply in special circumstances where the licensee cannot be given sole occupation of his home and therefore can only stay for a short period with minimum rights.

The right to quiet enjoyment of a property

Earlier, we saw that when a tenancy agreement is signed, the landlord is contracting to give quiet enjoyment of the tenants home. This means that they have the right to live peacefully in the home without harassment. The landlord is obliged not to do anything that will disturb the right to the quiet enjoyment of the home. The most serious breach of this right would be for the landlord to wrongfully evict a tenant.

......

Chapter 13

Carrying Out Repairs and Improvements To A Property

Repairs and improvements generally: The landlord and tenants obligations

Repairs are essential works to keep the property in good order. Improvements and alterations to the property, e.g. the installation of a shower. As we have seen, most tenancies are periodic, i.e. week-to-week or month-to-month. If a tenancy falls into this category, or is a fixed-term tenancy for less than seven years, and began after October 1961, then a landlord is legally responsible for most major repairs to the flat or house.

If a tenancy began after 15th January 1989 then, in addition to the above responsibility, the landlord is also responsible for repairs to common parts and service fittings. The area of law dealing with the landlord and tenants repairing obligations is the 1985 Landlord and Tenant Act, section 11.

This section of the Act is known as a covenant and cannot be excluded by informal agreement between landlord and tenant. In other words the landlord is legally responsible whether he or she likes it or not. Parties to a tenancy, however, may make an application to a court mutually to vary or exclude this section.

Example of repairs a landlord is responsible for:

- Leaking roofs and guttering.
- Rotting windows.
- Rising damp.
- Damp walls.
- Faulty electrical wiring.
- Dangerous ceilings and staircases.
- Faulty gas and water pipes.
- Broken water heaters and boilers.
- Broken lavatories, sinks or baths.

In shared housing the landlord must see that shared halls, stairways, kitchens and bathrooms are maintained and kept clean and lit.

Normally, tenants are responsible only for minor repairs, e.g., broken door handles, cupboard doors, etc. Tenants will also be responsible for decorations unless they have been damaged as a result of the landlord's failure to do repair.

A landlord will be responsible for repairs only if the repair has been reported. It is therefore important to report repairs in writing and keep a copy. If the repair is not carried out then action can be taken. Damages can also be claimed.

Compensation can be claimed, with the appropriate amount being the reduction in the value of the premises to the tenant caused by the landlord's failure to repair. If the tenant carries out the repairs then the amount expended will represent the decrease in value.

The tenant does not have the right to withhold rent because of a breach of repairing covenant by the landlord. However, depending on the repair, the landlord will not have a very strong case in court if rent is withheld.

Reporting repairs to landlords

The tenant has to tell the landlord or the person collecting the rent straight away when a repair needs doing. It is advisable that it is in writing, listing the repairs that need to be done. Once a tenant has reported a repair the landlord must do it within a reasonable period of time. What is reasonable will depend on the nature of the repair.

The tenants rights whilst repairs are being carried out

The landlord must ensure that the repairs are done in an orderly and efficient way with minimum inconvenience to the tenant If the works are disruptive or if property or decorations are damaged the tenant can apply to the court for compensation or, if necessary, for an order to make the landlord behave reasonably. If the landlord genuinely needs the house empty to do the work he/she can ask the tenant to vacate it and can if necessary get a court order against the tenant. A written agreement should be drawn up making it clear that the tenant can move back in when the repairs are completed and stating what the arrangements for fuel charges and rent are.

Can the landlord put the rent up after doing repairs?

If there is a service charge for maintenance, the landlord may be able to pass on the cost of the work(s).

Tenants rights to make improvements to a property

Unlike carrying out repairs the tenant will not normally have the right to insist that the landlord make actual alterations to the home. However, a tenant needs the following amenities and the law states that you should have:

- Bath or shower.
- Wash hand basin.
- Hot and cold water at each bath, basin or shower.
- An indoor toilet.

If these amenities do not exist then the tenant can contact the council's Environmental Health Officer. An improvement notice can be served on the landlord ordering him to put the amenity in.

Disabled tenants

If a tenant is disabled he/she may need special items of equipment in the accommodation. The local authority may help in providing and, occasionally, paying for these.

The tenant will need to obtain the permission of the landlord. If you require more information then contact the social services department locally.

Houses in multiple occupation (HMO)

A landlord has extra legal responsibilities if the house or flat shared with other tenants is a house in multiple occupation (HMO). The extra rules are there to reduce the risk of fire and to make sure that people living in shared houses or flats have adequate facilities. From

1st October 2018, all landlords who fall within the HMO category must be licensed by the local authority for the area. A home is an HMO if:

- 3 or more unrelated people live there as at least 2 separate households – for example, 3 single people with their own rooms, or 2 couples each sharing a room the 3 or more people living there share basic amenities, such as a kitchen or bathroom. The requirement for the property to cover three or more stories of a property has now been removed and it is estimated that this change will mean that some 177,000 rental properties will now be classed as HMOs.

A home is a large HMO if both of the following apply:
- At least 5 tenants live there, forming more than 1 household
- They share toilet, bathroom or kitchen facilities with other tenants

A household is either a single person or members of the same family who live together. A family includes people who are:
- married or living together - including people in same-sex relationships
- relatives or half-relatives, for example grandparents, aunts, uncles, siblings
- step-parents and step-children

An HMO could be a:
- house split into separate bedsits

150

- shared house or flat, where the sharers are not members of the same family
- hostel
- bed-and-breakfast hotel that is not just for holidays
- shared accommodation for students – although many halls of residence and other types of student accommodation owned by educational establishments are not classed as HMOs

Extra responsibilities of HMO landlords

Landlords of HMOs must make sure that:

- proper fire safety measures are in place, including working smoke alarms
- annual gas safety checks are carried out
- electrics are checked every 5 years
- the property is not overcrowded
- there are enough cooking and bathroom facilities for the number living there
- communal areas and shared facilities are clean and in good repair
- there are enough rubbish bins/bags
- Responsibility for repairs in HMOs
- A landlord is responsible for any repairs to communal areas of A home.

They are also responsible for repairs to:

- the structure and exterior of the house – including the walls, window frames and gutters

- water and gas pipes
- electrical wiring
- basins, sinks, baths and toilets
- fixed heaters (radiators) and water heaters

HMOs don't need to be licensed if they are managed or owned by a housing association or co-operative, a council, a health service or a police or fire authority.

Licences usually last for 5 years but some councils grant them for shorter periods. When deciding whether to issue or renew a licence, the council checks that:

- the property meets an acceptable standard. For example, it looks at whether the property is large enough for the occupants and if it is well managed
- the landlord is a 'fit and proper' person

Minimum bedroom size for HMOs
If a landlord applied for a HMO licence on or after 1 October 2018 or has renewed it since, bedroom sizes must be at least:

6.51 square metres for an adult
10.22 square metres for two adults
4.64 square metres for a child under 10 years old

Some councils may set higher standards for bedroom sizes. If a room is used as bedroom and doesn't meet the size requirement, the council may allow a landlord up to 18 months to make the room larger or move you to a different bedroom. The council can prosecute or fine a landlord if a bedroom is smaller than standards allow.

Landlord penalties for not having an HMO licence

A landlord can be fined and ordered to repay up to 12 months' rent if tenants live in a HMO that should be licensed but isn't. A tenants can apply for a rent repayment order within a year of the HMO being unlicensed, and also any housing benefit or universal credit tenants have used to help them pay rent will be reclaimed by the council.

Many people living in HMOs have an assured shorthold tenancy. If a tenant has an assured shorthold tenant and the HMO should be licensed but isn't, a landlord won't be able to evict tenants using a section 21 notice.

The council can prosecute landlords of HMOs, or any manager they have employed, if they break the law. In extreme cases, the council can take over the management of the property.

Safety generally for all landlords-the regulations

The main product safety regulations relevant to the lettings industry are:

- Gas safety
- The Gas safety (Installation and use) Regulations 1998
- The Gas Cooking Appliances (safety) Regulations 1989

- Heating Appliances(Fireguard) (safety) Regulations 1991
- Gas Appliances(Safety) Regulations 1995

All of the above are based on the fact that the supply of gas and the appliances in a dwelling are safe. A Gas Safety certificate is required to validate this.

Furniture Safety

Furniture and Furnishings (Fire) (Safety) Regulations 1988 and 1993 (as amended). Landlords and lettings agents are included in these regulations. The regulations set high standards for fire resistance for domestic upholstered furniture and other products containing upholstery.

The Regulations apply to any upholstered furniture manufactured after 1st January 1950 intended for use in a dwelling including:

- All types of upholstered seating including chairs, settees, padded stools and ottomans. Children's furniture, foot stools, sofa-beds, futons and other convertibles, bean bags and floor cushions nursery furniture and upholstered items designed to contain a baby or small child. Domestic upholstered furniture that is supplied in kit form for self-assembly. Second hand furniture Upholstered head-boards, footboards and side rails of beds.
- Furniture for use in the open air (garden and outdoor furniture) which is suitable for use in a dwelling (homes or caravans) such as conservatory furniture
- Upholstery in caravans (although not vehicles or boats) and Cane furniture which includes upholstery.

- Divans, bed-bases, mattresses, pillows, and mattress pads (toppers) scatter cushions and seat pads (FILLING MATERIAL ONLY)
- Permanent covers for furniture (textiles, coated textiles, leather etc) Loose and stretch covers for furniture. Covers for non-visible parts of furniture
- Foam and non-foam filling material for furniture

What items are not covered?
- Upholstered furniture manufactured before 1st January 1950
- Materials used solely to recover pre -1950 furniture
- Sleeping Bags
- Bed Clothes or Duvets
- Loose Mattress Covers
- Pillow Cases
- Curtains
- Carpets

Upholstered articles (i.e. beds, sofas, armchairs etc) must have fire resistant filling material. Upholstered articles must have passed a match resistant test or, if of certain kinds (such as cotton or silk) be used with a fire resistant interliner. The combination of the cover fabric and the filling material must have passed a cigarette resistance test.

The landlord should inspect property for non-compliant items before letting and replace with compliant items.

Electrical Safety

Electrical Equipment (Safety) Regulations 1994

Plugs and Sockets etc. (Safety) Regulations 1994.

Electrical hazards are also covered by the Housing Health and safety Rating System under the Housing Act 2004. In the case of commercial property and houses in multiple occupation there is a statutory duty under the Regulatory Reform Fire Safety Order 2005 for the responsible person (the property manager) to carry out annual Fire Safety Risk Assessments, which include electrical safety risks.

The Electrical Equipment Regulations came into force in January 1995. Both sets of regulations relate to the supply of electrical equipment designed with a working voltage of between 50 and 1000 volts ac. (or between 75 and 1000 volts dc.) the regulations cover all the mains voltage household electrical goods including cookers, kettles, toasters, electric blankets, washing machines, immersion heaters etc. The regulations do not apply to items attached to land. This is generally considered to exclude the fixed wiring and built in appliances (e.g. central heating systems) from the regulations. Lettings agents and landlords should take the following action:

Essential:

Check all electrical appliances in all managed properties on a regular fixed term basis. Remove unsafe items and keep a record of checks.

Recommended:

Have appliances checked by a qualified electrical engineer

Avoid purchasing second hand electrical items

There is no specific requirement for regular testing under the regulations. However, it is recommended that a schedule of checks, say on an annual basis, is put in place.

For more information on electrical safety visit www.landlordzone.co.uk/information/electrical-safety.

This is a particularly good site.

Tougher rules announced for electrical inspections for rented homes in the UK (January 2019)

Rules on electrical safety in the UK's private rented sector are being tightened to ensure mandatory electrical checks are carried out by competent and qualified inspectors. The tougher rules will mean greater protection for tenants and help drive up standards in the lettings sector.

Landlords will be legally required to ensure that the inspectors they hire to carry out safety inspections have the necessary competence and qualifications to do so with tough financial penalties for those who fail to comply. Ministers will also publish new guidance which sets out the minimum level of competence and qualifications necessary for those carrying out these important inspections, meaning both landlords and tenants can be assured their home is safe from electrical faults.

The availability of grants

There are a number of grants available to landlords at any one time which will enable improvements to take place to a property. One of the main grants is the Disabled facilities Grant. However, there are more and your local authority can tell you what is available.

Rgulations on Smoke and Carbon Monoxide detectors

From October 2015, all landlords, regardless of whether public or private sector, arequired to install working smoke and carbon monoxide alarms in their properties, on each floor. The carbon monoxide alarms need to be placed in high risk areas, i.e., where there are gas appliances such as boilers or fires. Carbon monoxide detectors will not be required in properties where there are no gas or solid fuel appliances. A civil penalty of up to £5,000 will apply to landlords who fail to comply with this legislation.

Obligations on Landlords to upgrade and maintain insulation

From April 2018, properties rented out in the private rented sector is required to have a minimum energy performance rating of E. The regulations apply to new lets and renewals of tenancies, and will apply to all existing tenancies on 1st April 2020. It will be against the law to rent a property which has a rating lower than E, unless there is an applicable exemption.

Legionnaire's disease

It is the responsibility of all landlords to undertake a risk assessment to prevent the spread of the Legionella bacteria, which can be found in a property's water systems and can lead to Legionnaires' disease if inhaled.

Legionnaires' disease is a pneumonia-like illness caused by Legionella bacteria and can be fatal. It is one of several conditions included within the Legionellosis group.

Although the risks are generally very low in residential property, health and safety legislation in the UK requires landlords to carry out risk assessments to control the exposure to tenants of Legionella.

The risk of Legionnaires' disease is likely to be higher in properties that are left empty and where water may be left to stand in both hot and cold systems, thus increasing the opportunity for the bacteria to multiply in the standing water.

As such, it is vital landlords ensure water systems are used at least once a week. And if a property is set to remain empty for several months, it may be worth draining the system to prevent the possibility of bacteria developing to unacceptable levels.

To minimise or eliminate the risk posed by Legionella, landlords should:

• Maintain cold water below 20 degrees C, as Legionella thrives in water between 20 and 45 degrees C
• Ensure showers and taps that are used infrequently - such as those in spare bedrooms - are periodically flushed through with running water
• Cover water tanks so mice, birds, insects and other creatures cannot gain access

• Remove unnecessary pipes, such as those leading to appliances that are no longer used

Signs of Legionella include:
• Cold water running warm
•Water that is discoloured or contains debris
• A malfunctioning boiler or hot water system

Sanitation health and hygiene generally
Local authorities have a duty to serve an owner with a notice requiring the provision of a WC when a property has insufficient sanitation, sanitation meaning toilet waste disposal.

They will also serve notice if it is thought that the existing sanitation is inadequate and is harmful to health or is a nuisance.

Local authorities have similar powers under various Public Health Acts to require owners to put right bad drains and sewers, also food storage facilities and vermin, plus the containing of disease.

The Environmental Health Department, if it considers the problem bad enough will serve a notice requiring the landlord to put the defect right. In certain cases the local authority can actually do the work and require the landlord to pay for it. This is called work in default.

****

Chapter 14

Repossessing A Property

Currently there is a consultation in progress concerning scrapping s21 notices, in order to attempt to try to regain more security in the private lettings market. Until then, the current s21 rules are outlined below.

Fast-track possession

A landlord cannot serve a s21 notice (Form 6A) on an assured shorthold tenant until after the first four months of a tenancy (if it is for a six month period). This brings the tenancy to an end on the day of expiry, i.e. on the day of expiry of the six month period,

Rules for Section 21 notices

If the tenancy started or was renewed on or after 1 October 2015 a landlord will need to use the new prescribed Section 21 notice Form (6a). Form 6A has replaced both S21 and S8 Notices although the Form still relates to S21 and S6 of the Housing Act.

Section 21 (Form 6A) pre-requisites

A landlord cannot serve a valid Form 6A notice if they have taken a deposit and not protected and/or served the prescribed information and/or they have failed to obtained a license for an HMO property which requires one. If the tenancy was in England and started or was renewed on or after 1 October 2015 a landlord must also have served on their tenant (and you should get proof of service for all these:

- an EPC
- a Gas Safety Certificate, and
- the latest version of the Government's "How to Rent" Guide.
- which deposit scheme the tenants deposit is in

Plus a landlord cannot serve a section 21 notice if their Local Authority has served one of 3 specified notices (the most important being an improvement notice) on them within the past six months in respect of the poor condition of the rental property.

Also, if the tenant complained about the issues covered by the notice prior to this – any Section 21 notice served since the complaint and before the Local Authority notice was served will also be invalid.

The notice period must not be less than two months and must not end before the end of the fixed term (if this has not ended at the time the landlord served their notice)

If this is a periodic tenancy where the period (rent payment period) is more than monthly (e.g., a quarterly or six month periodic tenancy), then the notice period must be at least one full tenancy period.

The notice period does not have to end on a particular day in the month, as was required under the old rules – the landlord just needs to make sure that the notice period is sufficient – minimum of 2 months.

On expiry of the notice, if it is the landlord's intention to take possession of the property then the tenants should leave. It is worthwhile writing a letter to the tenants one month before expiry reminding them that they should leave.

In the event of the tenant refusing to leave, then the landlord has to then follow a process termed 'fast track possession'. This entails filling in the appropriate forms (N5B) which can be downloaded from Her Majesty's Court Service Website www.justice.gov.uk.

Assuming that a valid Form 6A notice has been served on the tenant, the accelerated possession proceedings can begin and the forms completed and lodged with the court dealing with the area where the property is situated. In order to grant the accelerated possession order the court will require the following:

- The assured shorthold agreement
- The section 21 notice (Form 6A)
- Evidence of service of the notice

The best form of service of the Form 6A notice is by hand. If a landlord has already served the notice then evidence that the tenant has received it will be required. Having the correct original paperwork is of the utmost importance. Without this, the application will fail and delays will be incurred.

If the tenant disputes the possession proceedings in any way they will have 14 days to reply to the court. If the case is well founded and the paperwork is in order then there should be no case for defence. Once the accelerated possession order has been granted then this will need to be served on the tenant, giving them 14 days to vacate. In certain circumstances, if the tenant pleads hardship the court can grant extra time to leave, six weeks as opposed to two weeks. If they still do not vacate then an application will need to be made to court for a bailiffs warrant to evict the tenants.

Accelerated possession proceedings cannot be used against the tenant for rent arrears. It will be necessary to follow the procedure below.

An accelerated possession order remains in force for six years from the date it was granted.

Going to court to end the tenancy
There may come a time when a landlord needs to go to court to regain possession of their property. This will usually arise when the contract has been breached by the tenant, for non-payment of rent or for some other breach such as nuisance or harassment. As we have seen, a tenancy can be brought to an end in a court on one of the grounds for possession. However, as the tenancy will usually be an assured shorthold then it is necessary for the landlord to consider whether they are in a position to give two months notice and withhold the deposit, as opposed to going to court. The act of withholding the deposit will entail the landlord refusing to authorize the payment to the tenant online. This then brings arbitration into the frame. Deposit schemes have an arbitration system as an integral part of the scheme.

If a landlord decides, for whatever reason, to go to court, then any move to regain a property for breach of agreement will commence in the county court in the area in which the property is. The first steps in ending the tenancy will necessitate the serving of a notice of seeking possession Form 6A using one of the Grounds for Possession detailed earlier in the book. If the tenancy is protected then 28 days must be given, the notice must be in prescribed form and served on the tenant personally (preferably).

If the tenancy is an assured shorthold, which is more often the case now, then 14 days notice of seeking possession can be used. In all cases the ground to be relied upon must be clearly outlined in the notice. If the case is more complex, then this will entail a particulars of claim being prepared, usually by a solicitor, as opposed to a standard possession form.

A fee is paid when sending the particulars to court, which should be checked with the local county court. The standard form which the landlord uses for routine rent arrears cases is called the N119 and the accompanying summons is called the N5. Both of these forms can be obtained from the court or from www.courtservice.gov. When completed, the forms are sent in duplicate to the county court and a copy retained for for the landlord.

The court will send a copy of the particulars of claim and the summons to the tenant. They will send the landlord a form which gives them a case number and court date to appear, known as the return date. On the return date, the landlord should arrive at court at least 15 minutes early. Complainants can represent themselves in simple cases but are advised to use a solicitor for more contentious cases. If the tenant is present then they will have a chance to defend themselves.

A number of orders are available. However, if you a person has gone to court on the mandatory ground eight then if the fact is proved then they will get possession immediately. If not, then the judge can grant an order, suspended whilst the tenant finds time to pay.

In a lot of cases, it is more expedient for a landlord to serve notice-requiring possession, if the tenancy has reached the end of the period, and then wait two months before the property is regained. This saves the cost and time of going to court particularly if the ground is one of nuisance or other, which will involve solicitors.

In many cases, if landlords are contemplating going to court and have never been before and do not know the procedure then it is best to use a solicitor to guide the case through.

Costs can be recovered from the tenant, although this will depend on their means. If possession is regained midway through the contractual term then the landlord will have to complete the possession process by use of bailiff, pay a fee and fill in another form, Warrant for Possession of Land.

If a landlord has reached the end of the contractual term and wish to recover their property then a fast track procedure is available which entails gaining an order for possession and bailiff's order by post. This can be used in cases with the exception of rent arrears.

Chapter 15

Private Tenancies in Scotland

The law governing the relationship between private landlords and tenants in Scotland is different to that in England. Since the beginning of 1989, new private sector tenancies in Scotland were covered by the Housing (Scotland) Act 1988. Following the passage of this Act, private sector tenants no longer had any protection as far as rent levels were concerned and tenants enjoyed less security of tenure. However, **The Private Housing (Tenancies) (Scotland) Act 2016**, passed by the Scottish Parliament and coming into force on 1st December 2017 has changed the law concerning private tenancies in Scotland. The main provisions of the Act are outlined below.

The new Private Residential Tenancy

On 1 December 2017 a new type of tenancy came into force, called the private residential tenancy, it replaced assured and short assured tenancy agreements for all new tenancies from 1st December 2017. as a result of passing of The Private Housing (Tenancies) (Scotland) Act 2016. The new Scottish Private Residential Tenancy, (SPRT) will deliver improved security of tenure for tenants, including students in smaller purpose built and mainstream private rented accommodation, and also the power for local authorities to designate rent pressure zones within their jurisdiction. There will also be streamlined procedures for starting and ending a tenancy and a model agreement for landlords and tenants. The SPRT will become the standard tenancy agreement between residential landlords and tenants and will replace the most common types of residential tenancies in Scotland – the Short Assured Tenancy and the Assured Tenancy.

What changes has the private residential tenancy brought in?

Any tenancy that started on or after 1 December 2017 will be a private residential tenancy. These new tenancies will bring in changes and improvements to the private rented sector, including:

No more fixed terms - private residential tenancies are open ended, meaning a landlord can't ask a tenant to leave just because they have been in the property for 6 months as they can with a short assured tenancy.

Rent increases – a tenant's rent can only be increased once every 12 months (with 3 months notice) and if they think the proposed increase is unfair they can refer it to a rent officer.

Longer notice period - if a tenant has lived in a property for longer than 6 months the landlord will have to give them at least 84 days notice to leave (unless they have broken a term in the tenancy).

Simpler notices - the notice to quit process has been scrapped and replaced by a simpler notice to leave process.

Model tenancy agreement - the Scottish Government have published a model private residential tenancy that can be used by landlords to set up a tenancy.

Person already an assured/short assured tenant

If a tenant was already renting and were an assured or short assured tenant, on 1 December 2017, their tenancy will continue as normal until they or their landlord brings it to an end following the correct procedure. If a landlord then offers a tenant a new tenancy this will be a private residential tenancy.

What is a private residential tenancy?

A private residential tenancy is one that meets the following conditions:

- the tenancy started on or after 1 December 2017
- it is let to a person as a separate dwelling (home)
- the person must be an individual, meaning not a company
- it's their main or only home
- they must have a lease (although a written agreement not needed for a lease to exist)
- the tenancy is not a exemptions tenancy, as listed below.

Tenancy agreements

A person have the right to a tenancy agreement, which can be either a written or electronic copy, within 28 days of the start of the tenancy. The Scottish Government has published a model tenancy that a landlord can use to set up a tenancy. This tenancy plus a set of notes that a landlord must give to the tenant can be accessed at www.mygov.scot/tenancy-agreement-scotland.

This tenancy agreement contains certain statutory terms that outline both parties rights and obligations including:

- The tenant's and landlord/letting agent's contact details
- The address and details of the rented property
- The start date of the tenancy
- How much the rent is and how it can be increased

- How much the deposit is and information about how it will be registered
- Who is responsible for insuring the property.
- The tenant has to inform the landlord when they are going to be absent from the property for more than 14 days
- The tenant will take reasonable care of the property
- The condition that the landlord must make sure the property is in, including the repairing standard.
- That the tenant must inform the landlord the need of any repairs.
- That the tenant will give reasonable access to the property, when the landlord has given at least 48 hours notice

The process that the tenancy can be brought to an end
If a landlord uses the Scottish Government's' model tenancy they should also give the tenant the 'Easy Read Notes' which will explain the tenancy terms in plain English. If a landlord does not use the model tenancy they must give the tenant the private residential tenancy statutory terms: supporting notes, with their lease, which will explains the basic set of terms that a landlord has to include in the lease.

Rent Increases
The rent can only be increase once every 12 months and the landlord needs to give a tenant 3 months notice, using the correct notice of the rent increase. If the tenant doesn't agree to the rent increase they can refer it to the local rent officer. The referral to the rent officer must be done within 21 days of receiving the rent increase notice.

When a referral made to the rent officer, they will first issue a provisional order which will suggest the amount the rent can be increased. The tenant will have 14 days from the date the provisional order is issued to request a reconsideration. If the tenant requests a reconsideration the rent officer will look at it again before making a final order and telling them the date that the increase will take place.

Ending a tenancy

If a tenant wants to end the tenancy, then they will have to give the landlord 28 days notice in writing. The notice has to state the day on which the tenancy is to end, normally the day after notice period has expired.

The tenant can agree a different notice period with the landlord as long it is in writing. If there is no agreed notice then 28 days notice is the minimum required.

Landlord access

The tenant has to allow reasonable access to the landlord to carry out repairs, inspections, or valuations when:

- the landlord has given at least 48 hours' written notice, or
- access is required urgently for the landlord to view or carry out works in relation to the repairing standard

If a tenant refuses access the landlord can make an application to the First Tier Tribunal Housing and Property Chamber who may make an order allowing them access.

Getting repairs carried out

As with other tenancies, the landlord has to keep the property wind and watertight, and in a condition that is safe to live in. The landlord is also responsible for making sure that the property repairing standard is met. This is a basic level of repair that is required by law. The landlord must give the tenant information on the repairing standard and what they can do if the property does not meet it. If a tenant wants to carry out work on their home, such as redecorating or installing a second phone line, they will need to seek permission from the landlord. Some tenancy agreements will include a clause telling the tenant whether they can carry out this kind of work.

Can a tenant sublet or pass their tenancy on to someone else?

A tenant cannot sublet, take in a lodger or pass their tenancy on to someone else before first getting written agreement from the landlord.

Short assured and assured tenancies

Most residential lettings in Scotland made after 2 January 1989 and before 1st December 2017 are short assured tenancies. Those that aren't short assured are normally assured tenancies.

Short assured tenancies

This was the most common type of tenancy. A short assured tenancy makes it easier for a landlord to get a property than an assured tenancy. Before any agreement is signed, a landlord must use form AT5 to tell new tenants that the tenancy will be a short assured tenancy. (see appendix). If they don't, the tenancy will automatically be an assured tenancy. Initially, a short assured tenancy must be for 6 months or more. After the first 6 months, the tenancy can be renewed for a shorter period.

Assured tenancies

At the beginning of an assured tenancy, it will be classed as a 'contractual assured tenancy' for a fixed period of time. The tenancy automatically becomes a 'statutory assured tenancy' if:

- the landlord ends the tenancy by issuing a notice to quit (eg because they want to change the agreement) and the tenant stays in the property
- the fixed period covered by the tenancy comes to an end and the tenant stays in the property

There are different rights and responsibilities on both landlord and tenant depending on the type of assured tenancy.

Other types of tenancy

Most tenancies in Scotland issued before December 2017 are short assured or assured tenancies. The other tenancy types are:

- 'common law' tenancy - if a tenant shares their home as a lodger
- regulated tenancy - the most common form of tenancy before 1989
- agricultural tenancy
- crofting tenancy

Ending a Short assured tenancy

To get a property back, the landlord must give tenants a 'notice to quit' and a 'Section 33 notice'. For a short assured tenancy, the minimum notice period is 40 days if the tenancy is for 6 months or longer.

For a tenancy that is continuing on a month by month basis after the original period has ended, the notice period is a minimum of 28 days. The landlord must give 2 months notice when giving a Section 33 notice. They can issue both the notice to quit and Section 33 notice at the same time. (see appendix)

Other tenancy types (excluding the new private residential tenancy)

For other tenancy types the landlord must give at least:

- 28 days if the tenancy is for up to 1 month
- 31 days if the tenancy is for up to 3 months
- 40 days if the tenancy is for more than 3 months

Ending a tenancy early

A landlord can end a tenancy early if:

- the tenant breaks a condition of the tenancy agreement
- landlord and tenant agree to end the tenancy

If tenants don't leave

If the notice period expires and tenants don't leave the property, the landlord can start the process of eviction through the courts. A landlord must tell tenants of their intention to get a court order by giving them a 'notice of intention to raise proceedings' (AT6) (see appendix).

If tenants want to leave

The tenancy agreement should say how much notice tenants need to give before they can leave the property.

If the notice isn't mentioned in the tenancy agreement, the minimum notice a tenant can give is:

- 28 days if their tenancy runs on a month-to-month basis (or if it's for less than a month)
- 40 days if their tenancy is for longer than 3 months

Ending a tenancy early

Unless there's a break clause in the tenancy agreement, a landlord can insist that their tenants pay rent until the end of the tenancy. If tenants leave the property without giving notice, or before the notice has run out, they're still responsible for the property and the rent by law.

Houses in multiple occupation (HMOs)

If a tenant is living in a bedsit, shared flat, lodging, shared house, hostel or bed and breakfast accommodation it's likely that they will be living a house in multiple occupation or 'HMO'. A landlord will have an HMO if:

- tenants live with two or more other people, and
- they don't belong to the same family, and
- they share some facilities, e.g. a bathroom or kitchen, and
- the accommodation is their only or main home (if they are a student, their term-time residence counts as their main home).

If they live with a homeowner their family doesnt count as 'qualifying persons' when deciding whether or not a property is an HMO. So for example, if they share accommodation with the owner and one other unrelated lodger, they won't live in an HMO. If they live with the owner and two other unrelated lodgers, they will live in an HMO.

Is the landlord a fit and proper person to hold a licence?

Before it will grant an HMO licence, the council must check that the owner and anyone who manages the property (for example, a letting agent) don't have any criminal convictions, for example, for fraud or theft.

Is the property managed properly?

The council must check that the landlord respects tenants legal rights. They should be given a written tenancy agreement stating clearly what the landlord's responsibilities are, and what the tenants responsibilities are. This should cover things like rent, repairs and other rules. To manage the property properly, the landlord must:

- keep the property and any furniture and fittings in good repair
- deal with the tenant fairly and legally when it comes to rent and other payments, for example they:
- must go through the correct procedure if they want to increase the rent
- cannot resell the tenant gas or electricity at a profit
- not evict the tenant illegally
- make sure that their tenants don't annoy or upset other people living in the area.

Does the property meet the required standards?

To meet the standards expected of an HMO property:

- the rooms must be a decent size, for example, every bedroom should be able to accommodate a bed, a wardrobe and a chest of drawers.
- there must be enough kitchen and bathroom facilities for the number of people living in the property, with adequate hot and cold water supplies.
- adequate fire safety measures must be installed, for example the landlord must provide smoke alarms and self-closing fire doors and make sure there is an emergency escape route.
- all gas and electrical appliances must be safe.
- heating, lighting and ventilation must all be adequate.
- the property should be secure, with good locks on the doors and windows.
- there must be a phone line installed so that tenants can set up a contract with a phone company to supply the service.

Safeguarding Tenancy Deposits

A tenancy deposit scheme is a scheme provided by an independent third party to protect deposits until they are due to be repaid. Three schemes are now operating:

- Letting Protection Service Scotland
- Safedeposits Scotland
- Mydeposits Scotland

Landlord's legal duties

The legal duties on landlords who receive a tenancy deposit are:

- to pay deposits to an approved tenancy deposit scheme

- to provide the tenant with key information about the tenancy and deposit

Information about the schemes

Further details about the individual schemes are available on the individual scheme web sites below. Email addresses and telephone numbers are also included. All three schemes have a range of information available for both landlords (and their agents) as well as tenants and these include how landlords can join the schemes, how to submit deposits, how to ask for repayment of deposits and how the dispute resolution service will work.

Letting Protection Service Scotland

www.lettingprotectionscotland.com
Address:
The Pavilions
Bridgwater Road
Bristol
BS99 6BN
Email contact: events@lettingprotectionscotland.com
Telephone: 0330 303 0031

SafeDeposits Scotland
www.safedepositsscotland.com
Address:
Lower Ground
250 West George Street
Glasgow
G2 4QY

Email contact: info@safedepositsscotland.com
Telephone: 03333 213 136

Mydeposits Scotland
www.mydepositsscotland.co.uk
Address:
Premiere House
Elstree Way Borehamwood
Hertfordshire
WD6 1JH
Email contact: info@mydepositsscotland.co.uk
Telephone: 0333 321 9402

****

Useful websites

The Buying Process-general

The Local Government Association
www.local.gov.uk
Confederation of Scottish Local Authorities
www.cosla.gov.uk

Greater London Authority
www.london.gov.uk
The Environment Agency
www.environment-agency.gov.uk

www.homecheckuk.com

House Prices
Halifax www.halifax.co.uk
Nationwide www.nationwide.co.uk
Land Registry www.landreg.gov.uk
www.zoopla.co.uk
www.ourproperty.co.uk

Property Search Sites
www.hometrack.co.uk
www.rightmove.co.uk
www.zoopla.co.uk
www.primelocation.com
www.onthemarket.com

www.home.co.uk

findahood.com

propertynetwork.net

findproperty.co.uk

propertyauctionaction.co.uk

uniquepropertybulletin.co.uk

speedflatmating.co.uk (links those with rooms and those in need of a room)

The buying and selling process-law and taxation
The Law Society www.lawsoc.org.uk
The Council of Mortgage Lenders www.cml.org.uk
HM Customs and Revenue www.hmrc.gov

Scotland
Law Society of Scotland www.scotlaw.org.uk

Leasehold/freehold
Lease www.lease-advice.org
Association of Residential Managing Agents
www.arma.org.uk

Mortgage search sites/brokers
Money facts www.moneyfacts.co.uk
www.moneysupermarket.co.uk
www.moneynet.co.uk

New homes
NHBC www.nhbc.co.uk

Renting and Letting

Association of Residential Letting Agencies (ARLA)

Arbon House

6 Tournament Court

EdgeHill Drive

Warwick

CV34 6LG

Tel: 01926 496 800

Website: www.arla.co.uk

Email: help@propertymark.co.uk

Advice on taxation if you are considering letting out a property

www.which.co.uk/money/tax/income-tax/tax-on-property-and-rental-income/how-rental-income-is-taxed

www.gov.uk/guidance/income-tax-when-you-rent-out-a-property-working-out-your-rental-income

Auctions

www.primelocation.com

www.propertyauctions.com

propertyauctionaction.co.uk

****

Index

****